Exorcism:
Purging the Narcissist from Heart and Soul

By

H G Tudor

Exorcism: Purging the Narcissist from Heart and Soul

By

H G Tudor

Published by Insight Books

Introduction

Hello and welcome to Exorcism. My kind is often likened to a demon which invades both your life and your heart, mind and soul. Such is the degree to which we permeate your life, touching upon so many facets of it that it does indeed give the impression of being possessed by some demonic and evil force. The extent of our machinations and the repercussions that you feel from them are wide-spread, extensive and can be long-lasting. We appear regularly in your mind, invading your thoughts. You can feel us in your heart, causing it to quicken, to ache and to soar. Such is the intensity of our seduction of you that if feels like we have wrapped our soul around yours (if indeed we had one) and we will often use such words and those of a similar nature to convey this sense of uniting together, two becoming one and not knowing where one of us ends and the other begins. The deep and intense seduction is akin to us taking you over and once we have achieved that total control, then the terrible and unpleasant machinations begin. The abuse commences and with you in our grip, we deploy all manner of manipulations to achieve our aims. We appear to be everywhere. We are by your side, we infect your dreams, we ring and message and then disappear when we engage in one of our frequent silent treatments. Even when we are not physically next to you, our presence remains. We make your mind race with thoughts and anxiety. We dominate your every waking moment and disrupt your sleep.

Once we throw you to one side or if you manage to escape us through the implementation of no contact, our possession of you does not end there. One might hope that having been freed of the concept of being in some kind of relationship with you, whether as intimate partner, family member, friend or colleague, that our presence would drift away and our hold on you would loosen. That is not the case. We repeatedly try and exert further control over you through the application of hoovers. We remain within you as a consequence of the massive impact we made on your life through our seduction and subsequent devaluation and discard. People meet thousands of people, maybe even more in some instances, during their lives. Few of those people have any lasting impact. Yes, they may be long-standing friends, someone who inspired a person, someone who guided them through their formative years, someone who put them on the right path in terms of their career aspirations. It may be the case that somebody was a dependable rock (certainly not one of our kind) who appeared in somebody's hour of need and supported them through some kind of crisis and their compassion has left their mark. For the most part however people drift together and then move on without leaving any lasting impression. This is not the case when someone encounters our kind.

You know better than anybody what the dramatic impact is of becoming engaged with one of our kind. What you need to understand is why do we have such an impact and what can you do about it? What is it that enables us to have such an effect upon you?

I am not a healer. There are many other people who engage in such work as a consequence of their profession, their empathic qualities and/or the fact that they too have experienced our kind and they have learned from the experience in terms of being able to move on and recover. I am a narcissist. As a consequence of the natural awareness that I have and that which has been brought to me as a result of my ongoing treatment I am able to deliver information to you. This information is from my perspective. This is what I think. This is what I do. This is my reasoning. It is rare to receive such a perspective, but it is mine. I will give you the information which you can then, if you so choose, apply to your understanding. That is a matter for you. I am not here to tell you what to do. You are an adult and you are in charge of yourself. I am not here to take you by the hand and console you, empathise and be compassionate. Of course I can feign all of that, I have watched and observed many people do it, so I am fully aware of my capability to manufacture what appears to be kindness and caring, but I do not feel it. What I will do is give you information which you will rarely receive from elsewhere and

4

then you can decide if you wish to apply this to assist your understanding of the situation. It is not comfortable reading what I have to write. I avoid being gratuitous in order to maintain our famed economy of effort, but I take the view that it better for you to receive the bold and uncompromised reality of what my kind and me do.

I know the effects that our behaviour has on those who entangle with us. I have seen it many time from those who I have ensnared. I have listened to their protestations and explanations of how it makes them feel, carefully storing this information and these responses in order to maximise my methodology for my own benefit. I know what I am and I am gaining understanding of what it means to be what I am. I am prepared to share this with you. I know the extent to which we affect you and how hard it is for you, even when the relationship has been ended in the traditional sense (because from our perspective the relationship only ends when one of us dies – if there is a chance to obtain more fuel from you at some point we will take it) for you to purge us from within you. It is as if we have become part of your DNA. You think about us repeatedly, your emotions are still affected by us, you long and pine for us even though you know how badly we have treated you. You eventually begin to understand what has happened to you, but the emotional fall-out continues. This is what causes the most pain and you just want to stop that feeling. I know full well what it is like because my victims have told me in detail just what it is like and I have extensive experience of others who may not be victims but they too have shared how we affect them post-discard or post-escape.

It is a terrible and tortuous time for you and you just want the sensation to go away so you can move forward. It is achievable. I am going to explain why that is so from my perspective because I know what we do to infect you with this sensation in the first place. Who better to engage with for the purposes of identifying a way forward than the person who caused the issue in the first place? By explaining to you what we do and why it is so effective you will gain understanding. This understanding in itself is crucial in tackling the emotional impact you suffer from entangling with us. Moreover, armed with this understanding you will then identify the array of actions you can take to tackle the emotional impact. I detail many of them later in this book and of course you will also find others, those who are more of the "healing" nature than I, who will provide you with further information to assist you in your recovery. What I will provide you with however is the understanding that is necessary to purge the effects of our infection from your heart and soul. I put it there in the first place. I am therefore best-placed to tell you why it is there, why it affects you in the way that it does and most of all what you can do about it.

I do not engage in detailed scientific explanations. I am not a man of science. That is for others to do. I find that such esoteric labelling has a purpose within the relevant scientific disciplines but for the purpose of communication and getting the message across in an effective manner, such lengthy explanations and cumbersome labels are unnecessary. I provide you with the insight from the perspective of my kind and me. Our conduct is calculated and necessary. The Lesser and Mid-Range of our kind do not know nor understand why they do as they do in infecting you in this way. The Greater of our kind know that we do it and also we understand why this is the case. We know full well that we must infect you, we know how to do it, what works best and because of this awareness we also know what you can do to counter it. There is undoubtedly science at work in this process because our infection of you relies on reinforcement, programming, conditioning and addiction. I have little doubt that one can read about the scientific explanation as to why you are addicted to our kind, in terms of what happens to you chemically and changes to your brain etc. There is much validity in that, however, what I am providing you with is how we go about causing that addiction, why you become addicted, what it is about you that provides such a fertile breeding ground for such addiction, how we know about this and exploit it to our advantage and ultimately, what you can do about it. By understanding addictive infection from our perspective it will assist you considerably.

Thank you for reading this book. You will find it interesting and insightful but most of all it will provide you with the capacity, if you so choose, to purge your heart and mind of our kind. You may feel like we have possessed you. You may feel like every fibre of your being has been touched by our once glorious and then malevolent touch. You can feel us in and around you. Now it is time to banish the demon. It is time to undertake your exorcism.

The Current Position

It is worthwhile considering the position that you currently find yourself viz a viz the narcissist who swept in to your life and caused such chaos. This is appropriate because in order to undertake the relevant purging you need to have got yourself to a certain place.

If you are in the throes of being seduced by a narcissist and you are one of the very rare breed who realises this is what is actually happening, then it is too early for you to perform the necessary purging. You are still in the grip of the marvellous golden period when everything is wonderful. It is extremely unusual for a victim to realise that they are being seduced by a narcissist. This is because most people do not know what we are and even fewer would recognise us at work. Most people just think that they have found their soul mate and someone who is infatuated in them and loving. This is not regarded as a bad thing because it feels brilliant. It is a bad thing for you because you are being charmed and pulled into a false reality which will ultimately turn sour for you. If someone has drawn your attention to the fact you are being seduced and you have seen and most of all **paid attention** to the various red flags that are flying your first step is to disengage from the person who has been seducing you. Remove yourself and reject all attempts from them to continue the seduction. They will try to keep going but a firm line will eventually cause them to go and pursue somebody else because they need the fuel that is provided from a charmed victim during seduction. If you are not providing this, then we need to get it from someone else and we will break off the seduction and go after somebody else. If you somehow know what is happening (usually because somebody observing has alerted you to it and you have amazingly listened to them) and you halt your seduction, then you have had a close shave and a fortunate escape before suffering the worst of what we are. This cessation may have taken place sufficiently early before any addiction has taken hold of you. If that is the case, then other than for your interest you need not apply the principles contained in this book. The reality is however that those people who manage to break off from a narcissist's seduction at such an early stage are extremely rare.

It may be the case that you were sufficiently hooked on the relevant narcissist who entered your life but you managed to escape before the devaluation began. Similarly, you have avoided the worst but the addictive quality has taken hold of you and you detached with reluctance and a whole host of unanswered questions. You may find yourself thinking often about this person and wondering what might have been, even though you are reliably and repeatedly told that you did the best thing in getting away. Although you have escaped the worst, this nagging itch remains and therefore you need to purge this sensation.

If you are in the throes of the devaluation there is little doubt that you wish to purge our effects from you but you have a much more pressing requirement. You need to escape us. You cannot successfully exorcise our kind from your life when you are caught in the devaluation, still bound to us in a variety of ways. Accordingly, if you are reading this book when you are in this stage, do not despair because its content will prove invaluable to you in due course, but for now you must focus on either escaping us totally by going no contact (and to that end I recommend to you my book **No Contact : How to Beat the Narcissist**) or if you are unable to completely free yourself from a relationship with a narcissist for whatever reason (timing, finances, children, illness etc.) then you need to learn how to manage and counter the manipulative effects of our machinations by addressing each type of manipulation as it occurs. On that basis I recommend you read **Escape: How to Beat the Narcissist**. Secure your escape either in the total sense or from the worst effects of the manipulations and then address the issue of purging us.

Most likely I should imagine that you find yourself in a position of being post-escape or post-discard. Post escape is where you have managed to call time on the relationship, you have implemented no contact and you have managed to resist the inevitable hoovers. You may well be in a vulnerable position still as you seek to recover but you are progressing in the correct direction. In order to fend off the hoovers I recommend **Black Hole: The Narcissistic Hoover** in conjunction with applying the principles contained in this book. Post discard is where we have callously thrown you to one side. This is the darkest and most despairing place that our victims find themselves. We may have left you alone for the time being (but understand there will be hoovers on the way at some point) and you are utterly bewildered as to what has happened to you. The positive however is that you are not physically proximate to our kind following this discard (or perhaps more accurately this dis-engagement since we will come back for you).

Whether you are in a post-discard or post-escape position this is when the content of this book is at its most valuable. The relationship (from your perspective) has ended whether you wanted it to or not. You are not tightly bound to us and no contact is in place (either because you have instigated it or because we don't want anything to do with you) and this is when you feel the terrible after-effects of having been ensnared with our kind. The devaluing manipulations of silent treatments, triangulation, gas lighting and a dozen more abuses may have stopped but out hold over you remains. You remain infected by us. It is at this juncture you want to get us out of your heart and soul and this is where this book has it greatest applicability.

Accordingly, assess where you are in relation to the narcissistic individual you became involved with. You need to be in a position of no longer having any (or minimal) contact with them so that you are then in the best place to tackle the after effects which linger as a consequence of our infection.

What are you seeking to purge?

Accordingly, since you are now in a position to tackle the after effects of being ensnared by us, what are those after effects and what is it that needs to be purged? There are many consequence of entangling with our kind and it is one of the products of such entanglement that you are seeking to purge, but what is it precisely that you are seeking to address and remove from yourself? There are many downsides to finding that you have been ensnared by us and it is worth beginning by addressing what some of those downsides are as we clarify them in pursuit of the actual things that you want to be rid of. When I refer to the need to purge us from your heart and soul, there are certain after effects which are clearly devastating to you but I do not include them as items which need to be purged. For example, following your entanglement with us, you may well find the after effects including the following: -

- Financial destitution
- Loss of home;
- Difficulties in terms of arrangements concerning children;
- Employment problems;
- PTSD or C-PTSD
- Loss of relationships (friends, colleagues, family)
-

Whilst any of these is not to be diminished in terms of their impact on a victim of our kind, these are not after effects which are directly linked to the need to exorcise us from you. However, these effects will be improved as an indirect consequence of the purging and the fact that you are able to move forward.

- Finance. You will be able to focus on organising your finances, confronting difficult scenarios with greater confidence and improve your finances through being able to work.
- Home. You will be able to organise accommodation with a greater sense of purpose and rebuild once the shackles of restraint have been removed.
- Children. You will find it easier to care for them and also more capable in terms of any interaction that must take place with the other party involved in the children's lives. You will be able to handle any court proceedings surround this more effectively.
- Employment. You will be able to focus on your job far better or focus on getting a job.
- PTSD – your situation will be improved by the removal of the infection which will have a knock on effect on many of the symptoms that arise in respect of PTSD
- Relationships. You will be able to dedicate time to those relationships which may have deteriorated or even been loss as a consequence of the effects of your involvement with our kind. Your will want to engage in these relationships and respond in a more productive manner.

Accordingly, some of the effects which arise from being ensnared by us are indirectly improved as a consequence of the purging that will take place, but it is not those after effects I have detailed above which are part of the purging. That is something else.

You may be physically rid of us, but what needs to be purged is something additional. Those items which need to be purged are what I describe as the Aftermath Effects. These are also as a direct consequence of your involvement with us. It is these effects which are the focus of what needs to be purged.

There are several Aftermath Effects.

The Illusion

One of the hardest things for you to tackle and understand, is that what just happened to you felt very real but was based on a fallacy. We did not love you. Not in the way you understand love to be. We fabricated this golden period. Everything and I mean everything contained within it was a lie. This is very hard to accept but accept it you must.

You fell in love with an illusion. You fell hard and deep for something which never existed. The golden days that we created together were the twisted reflections of my manipulative hold over you. I know how anxious you were to try to recover the golden period. You poured your beautiful heart into securing the impossible. I know that my silences, my verbal violence, the cheating and the lies, my perfidious control of you was brutal, malicious and devastating. I understand that the whole avalanche of manipulative techniques I applied to you, in savage wave after insidious wave crushed your self-esteem, mauled your sanity and shattered your world. This brutality was nothing compared to the aftermath.

For now, you have slipped away from my tight, choking grip. I know however that you sit looking from the window where you used to watch for me strolling up the driveway, a bouquet in my hands and the pain still wracks you as you remember how you fell in love with someone who was not real. Memory after memory stirs from within, an endless loop of 'best of' moments that you want to stop remembering but you cannot. It hurts yet you still want to remember because even as the pain rises in your chest, you still feel the flicker of your love for me and you still cherish that. Like the drug addict, you know that line of cocaine is no good for you but still you need to snort it. The cold silences may no longer chill our living room. The sting of my slap across your cheek has long since faded. The barbed comments I fired your way each day have lost their power to wound. All of that has gone. The one lingering, tortuous pain that still sits deep within you is the knowledge that you were in love with an illusion No matter how much you discuss it with your friends, the earnest hours with your therapist and the pile of books about healing that are stacked up besides your favourite chair (which I always tried to sit in before you), none of them help take away that awful aching.

You can manage the shame of being fooled. You take a strange pride in having given your all to such a despicable person because that is the person you are. Honest, decent and a provider of unconditional love. You do not want that to change. You do not want to lose the empathy for which you are renown. The battered bank balance will repair (eventually) and the dosage of the medication will come down (your doctor has said as such in soothing tones). The strength of character which made me choose you means you can deal with all of these things. The one thing that will never leave is that deep-seated pain that you loved a ghost. Your head will eventually accept what happened, that you were charmed, entranced and enchanted and you never stood a chance. That was why you were chosen. Emotionally, you will never lose that dull ache as you sit and reminisce about our time together and how wonderful being in love with me was. Your heart will never accept that it was not real.

That crack, that fracture, that tiny chink that remains from your frenetic and devastating time with me shall always remain. It is through it that I can return as I slip, shadow like into your heart through that unhealed wound. That is why we did what we did; so we always had a way back in. I placed deep inside you a powerful mixture which when activated by your thoughts about me, your reflection on what happened and any consideration of what we did, had and said, will awaken the addictive qualities which caused you to fall for the illusion in the first place. It is a potent and dangerous mixture. For all of the strength that you exhibit through never taking a call from us, from changing email accounts, from burning the pictures and changing mobile numbers, you are never truly safe. Yes, you manage to evade the snaking tendrils that we uncoiled to try to haul you back under our spell. You will have to maintain that vigilance for the rest of your life. Our polluting influence, through this mixture, if ever allowed near you again, will creep and trickle through the hole that will never seal. You are consigned to a lifetime of wariness and maintain your defences because that damage is permanent.

You will always be in love with the person you thought I was.

The fact that you fell in love (and did so deeply and completely) with an illusion has the after effect of what I describe as **The Illusion Questions.** These are a set of questions which go round and round in your mind and because you (as an empathic individual always want to know the truth and receive answers) it prevents you from moving forward.

The creation of this illusion serves many purposes to us. It draws you to us, it binds you to us, it causes you to give us fuel and it also causes you to not give up when the devaluation begins but fight to return to this illusory golden period. It also allows the Illusion Questions to exist as an aftermath effect of being ensnared by us.

What are those questions?

Surely he must have loved me, it felt so real?

Some of it must have been real, I mean what about (insert example which you use to convince yourself that it was real to some degree)

Why would someone do that to me?

What is the point of behaving like that?

How did she manage to do it for as long as she did?

Did he not feel any love for me at all?

But everything he did looked and felt like love, it must he been that surely?

No, he loved me, something just went wrong and we can sort it out. I just need to work out what it is and the only way I can do that is to ask him about it?

These and similar questions are all part of the Illusion Questions which are designed to have you struggle to accept it really was an illusion (thus preventing you from moving on and making you susceptible to being hoovered as you want to engage with us again). This is a deliberate consequence of creating this illusion. It is used to ensnare you and keep a hold of you.

Total Dedication

The encompassing nature of our illusory love for you during the seduction and then the strenuous efforts which you then went to, to get back to the golden period when the devaluation occurred, means that you gave your total dedication to your relationship with us. You loved like you never have loved before, you submitted, you acquiesced, you helped, you soothed, you compromised again and again, you allowed your own character to be eroded, you let go of your interests, you let friends and family slip away, you poured your everything into the idea of you and I. You believed in it above everything else because that is the type of person that you are, as a love devotee. Every conceivable resource that belonged to you, both tangible and intangible was utilised for the purpose of our relationship. You gave it everything.

In the aftermath you are left feeling spent, exhausted and emptied by this Herculean effort on your part. You allowed (because you were conned) yourself to be swept up by our love bombing. You held nothing back. You did not keep a piece of your heart or your soul from us, but laid it all out in front of you because you were convinced by our illusory love that this was the right thing to do. You clung on through the horrendous treatment of the devaluation, unwilling to give up on us, hoping to resurrect the golden period and make everything well again. You tried and tried and tried.

Now you are left with the knowledge that you gave everything and you have been left with nothing. It is worse than placing everything you own on red and it coming up black. You know you made a total investment in a relationship and your return has been nothing.

The sensation that this leaves you with is devastating and long-lasting. It also brings with it a set of questions which occupy your mind.

What happened to me?

Is that it?

How did I end up here?

I don't understand what happened to everything I gave?

Why wasn't it enough for him?

Why didn't he tell me what he actually wanted?

How did I let that happen?

Why have I been left with nothing after everything that I have done?

The Fool

A further Aftermath Effect which is linked to the concept of Total Dedication is the feeling that you are a fool. You eventually realise that you have been conned. You have been duped by a convincing, probably the most convincing fraudster. You like to think you are intelligent, aware, sensible and independent but you have been totally had over. What is worse, now with 20/20 hindsight you are able to see the massive red flags that were flying. You can see the red lights flashing and hear those klaxons blaring. It all seems to obvious. Similar to the Illusion Questions you are also faced with the Foolish Questions which occupy your mind night and day.

How did I not spot what he was?

How could I have been so stupid?

I feel such an idiot. Why did I not trust my instinct?

How could I be fooled in this way?

Why am I such an idiot for believing him?

Why didn't I listen to (insert name of well-meaning advisor who tried to warn you)?

Why didn't somebody warn me?

Why didn't I pay more attention when I felt something wasn't right?

What is wrong with me?

Just like the Illusion Questions, these questions will go round and round in your mind as you beat yourself up. Part of our behaviour is not to give you answers. We know you want answers. Most people do, but you, as an empathic individual want them more than average people. Since we know this, our behaviour is engineered to cause you to ask lots of questions of yourself and of us but not to provide you with those answers. This means we prevent you from moving forward and keep you wanting to interact with us (thus making you vulnerable to hoovers) so you can try and achieve some answers. The sense of shame and embarrassment is considerable and this combines with the repeated questions which whirl around in your head.

The Loss of Trust

Related to the issue of total dedication is the loss of trust which arises from being involved with our kind. It is devastating the manner in which your capability to trust is affected by what we have done to you. You operate always from a position of trust, it is one of your empathic traits and you expect the same of those that you deal with. We not only tear your trust apart, we set fire to it and trample the ash into the ground. We seriously affect your ability to trust people as a whole but especially within the context of a romantic relationship. In common with the other Aftermath Effects, this damaging effect of ours results in further questions which will occupy your mind.

How can I trust anyone again?

What if I meet another narcissist?

How will I be able to tell if someone is false?

How can I tell if someone is genuine?

What do I need to do to protect myself from having my trust abused again?

Am I better off not being with someone so I won't have my trust abused?

The Longing

Whilst there is no doubt that the other Aftermath Effects are bad enough, it is perhaps this one that causes substantial problems for our victims. You know what we are, be it abuser or more specifically a narcissistic individual. You understand to some extent the abuse that you have been put through. You may not recognise every manipulation that was applied to you, but you know only too well the hurt the fear, the sick sensation and the upset that you experienced. Yet, notwithstanding your head telling you all of this, you are beset by that desire to be with us again. You want to see us. You want to know what we are doing. You want to know who we are with and where we have been. You physically ache for our presence as everything feels so empty and vacant without us. You will of course make excuses for our devaluation and discard of you, since you have been conditioned to do so by our treatment of you. You will focus on the golden period since you want that again and you want it so, so much. You just want to see that smile again, hold our hand, hear us laugh and kiss us. Just another night together to stop this aching, this longing, this horrible pain. We know very well what you suffer from for we have heard it described and seen how you behave. You know that you should not be with us but you cannot help but feel like this. Just like the other Aftermath Effects this one comes with a whole host of questions.

Why do I feel like this?

Why won't it stop?

Why can't I stop wanting her?

Why can't I stop thinking about him?

Why does it hurt so much?

Will this feeling going away?

Why can I not get him out of my head?

Why does he have this hold over me?

The cumulative effect of these Aftermath Effects is to cause you to keep asking the same questions again and again and focusing on us rather than concentrating on yourself. This is what we want. We want it to be about us. We do not want you focusing on your needs because if you do that then you might do something which helps yourself and thus in turn escape us. This cumulative effect is known as the Wrong Focus.

The actions we take against you when we are with you are always designed to impact upon you both then and at a later stage. The examples of this are legion. For instance, during our seduction of you we are placing and creating Ever Presence which we will rely on post-discard or post-escape in order to keep you susceptible to longing for us (as well as many other things) so that hoovering you becomes so much easier. Consider also, again through seduction, how the provision of compliments, a supposedly perfect love, great sex, happy times together and so forth is achieved. All of this is done so we can not only bind you to us but then it provides us with the material to cause you to plummet far when we withdraw all of that from you. So much of what we do has an immediate and a later effect. One of these effects is to create in you the concept of the Wrong Focus.

If you have managed to escape us or more likely you have been discarded, we know (because we have engineered this to happen) that there are so many things that you will be doing and that you will do, which collectively we consider as the Wrong Focus. This is designed to suit our purposes and without fail it always happens following an entanglement with our kind. This is as a consequence of two factors. The first is because of the way that we have treated you because it does not make sense, lacks logic and is so confusing. That in itself creates so many questions and considerations which form the Wrong Focus. Secondly, it is in your nature to ask these questions and also to want answers to them because one of your traits is a need to know the truth. Some people (although of course we would never target them) might just brush themselves down and move forwards without a backwards glance in our direction. Those people have no interest in working out was happened and have no desire to know the truth. Those people are of no use to us and will not be chosen for targeting and seduction. Instead, it is people like you who are susceptible to our overtures and possess those traits which mean that the happening of the Wrong Focus is as guaranteed as the sun rising in the east.

So, what are the constituent parts of the Wrong Focus? There are many indeed and here are thirty for your consideration and information.

1. You will wonder why we treated you so terribly after we were so wonderful to you.
2. You will want to know how we could have just left you like that after everything that you did for us?
3. You will be perplexed as to how we are able to move on to somebody else so soon after being with you, especially since we said that you and I were soulmates and would be together until the end of time?
4. What are we doing with our new acquisition?
5. How are they better than you?
6. Are we happy with that person now?
7. What has that person got that you haven't?
8. She doesn't even seem like our type so why on earth have we chosen her?
9. You spend your time on "Ex Watch" as you stalk our social media (and that of the new target) to see what we are doing together, what we are saying to one another and looking for any signs of trouble in this new relationship.

10. You want our new relationship to fail so you feel better and validated because the same thing has happened to the new target as it did to you.

11. You feel a need to prove that you are happy (even though you are not) and that you need us to know that this is the case. You consider ways in which you can convey this message to us.

12. You wonder what you could do to win us back.

13. You wonder what mistakes were made that caused the relationship to fall apart.

14. You begin to imagine what is going on in between those four walls, that you knew so well once upon a time, becoming fixated with considering what is happening.

15. You relive the day you had with us and think about whether we are doing the same things with the new person as we did with you.

16. You want us to explain why we did what we did?

17. You try to make sense of what has happened but you cannot. This does not, however, stop you from running the whole relationship through your head over and over again as you seek to find answers.

18. You sit and ask yourself are we thinking about you?

19. You ruminate on whether we miss you at all.

20. Does she kiss us like you did?

21. Do we love her more than we loved you?

22. Have we kept the gifts you gave us?

23. Why have we deleted all the pictures of you on social media?

24. Why haven't we deleted all the pictures of you on social media?

25. Why are we saying those things about you to other people?

26. Do we feel bad at the way that we treated you?

27. Why does it feel like no matter what you do we always seem to win?

28. Will we ever speak to you again?

29. Will our friends and family still acknowledge you after everything that has happened?
30. What if she is "the one"?

You spend so much time occupied with these thoughts. They dominate your mind. You replay scenarios in order to try and answer these questions. You sit and discuss these questions with friends and family who do their best to be supportive but they do not have the answers. You will not receive any answers from them that will satisfy you because ultimately you want those answers to come from us and we know that. That is why we will not provide them to you.

You will have immediately noticed what all of the above thirty points have in common. They are all about us. This is deliberate. We want everything to be all about us. We want that during seduction, during devaluation and post escape or post discard. It always has to revolve around us and the creation of so many questions arising out of our treatment of you is a deliberate consequence which is designed to have you focus on us.

This paralyses you.

This repeats the pain.

This holds you back.

This keeps you susceptible to the hoover that will come.

This is what we want.

We want you to focus on us.

You need to focus on you.

But you will always apply the wrong focus. By applying the principles in this book and exorcising us from heart and soul you will prevent the Aftermath Effects and in turn you will destroy the Wrong Focus.

Accordingly, in terms of purging your narcissist from your heart and soul, it is the Aftermath Effects which need to be exorcised. You need to banish the following: -

1. **The Illusion**
2. **The Total Dedication**
3. **The Fool**
4. **The Loss of Trust**
5. **The Longing**

It is these five Aftermath Effects which are central to your continued pain and paralysis. It is these five that must be addressed in order to bring about a successful purge. In order to banish them in an effective fashion you need to understand how these five categories of Aftermath Effects are achieved.

How are the Aftermath Effects Achieved?

There are five things that our kind does in order to bring about these Aftermath Effects. It is not a case that doing a particular thing will cause, for example, the effect of Total Dedication, but rather each of these five actions will cause the Aftermath Effects. The effectiveness of these effects (something which I discuss in greater detail below) relies on reinforcement. The repeated application of certain actions and behaviours which results in the addictive qualities being created. The repeated layering of these behaviours essentially becomes habit forming so that you lose the need to link the action with the effect in a conscious way, but rather it happens unconsciously, as a matter of reaction. Thus, we do not rely on just one act to create all five of the effects but instead we do one thing, then another, then a third, then a fourth and a fifth in order to ensure through this repetition that the effects are well and truly applied to you and become a part of you. We learn through repetition and reinforcement. A cow in a field receives an electric shock if it touches the fence. After two or three shocks, the cow realises that touching the fence always results in pain and therefore it will stop doing it. Children learn their time tables through the repetition of five times five equals twenty-five, six times five equals thirty and so on. When you revised for your examinations you most likely re-read your notes and work throughout the year, wrote it down again, repeated key points, such as dates, equations, theories, laws and such like again and again until your found that as soon as someone asked,

"When was the Battle of White Mountain?"

You answered, without needing to think.

"1620."

We understand that repetition is fundamental in ensuring that these effects are ingrained deep inside of you. By way of example, why do you think that during the love-bombing period we sent you a delightful text every morning at 7am? We did it every day without fail. Yes, this was to seduce you by writing something romantic and complimentary, so you felt wonderful and we appeared marvellous. Yes, it was designed to bind you tighter to us. It was also done so that you became conditioned to receive a little boost at 7am, a good start to the day. It created expectation and after weeks of this, you did not wake up and see the text message had arrived from us and think,

"I wonder what this is?"

Your heart lifted and you felt good as soon as you saw that text message in your inbox because you automatically knew that it would contain some loving words, some expression of devotion or some compliment about how wonderful you are. You did not have to think what was contained in the message, you automatically felt good as soon as you saw it.

By the same token, when those texts stopped it created anxiety and longing. You had been conditioned to expect them and when no such text appeared, that instant hit of delight was denied to you and you longed for it, added to which you became anxious as to why it was not there. When one omission became two and then three, the effect of the conditioning really began to hurt as your heart longed for that hit of delight it had become so accustomed to receiving and which was now being denied to you.

Accordingly, whilst we may take the view that one particular behaviour or event might cause these five after effects, we know that we stand a far better chance of creating deeper and longer lasting Aftermath Effects through the application of repetition and thus we utilise five methods of embedding these effects. These are the Causal Actions.

1. The Golden Period

The first method of causing of the Aftermath Effects is the golden period. This is the time from when our seduction of you commences until the devaluation begins. The duration of the golden period varies dependent on the capacity of the victim to provide potent positive fuel, the role that the victim has vis a vis the narcissist and the nature of the relevant narcissist. It may sometimes just be a few months and in other instances it may stretch to many years. It is usually the case that the golden period will be longer for those who are deemed to be supplementary sources of fuel compared to someone who is made the primary source of fuel. An outer circle friend may experience a long-lasting golden period because the narcissist recognises the value in maintaining that for the purposes of the façade. In addition, the outer circle friend has less frequent interaction than a primary source, with the narcissist, with the effect that the risk of the outer circle friend triggering a discard by the narcissist is much reduced. Accordingly, as a general rule, the golden period will last longer for those who are secondary and tertiary sources of fuel, rather than the primary source of fuel (which is usually an intimate partner).

Whatever length of time the golden period lasted for, the effect of the golden period is undoubted. In a normal relationship, I understand that the process of falling in love with another is a gradual process whereby both parties spend time with one another over an extended period as they get to know one another. There is a honeymoon period which embodies the sensations of falling in love, excitement and anticipation and then the relationship settles into something deep-seated, stable and enduring. None of this process is applicable to the means by which we engage with our victims. The honeymoon period may seem wonderful to the two people enjoying it, but it pales when compared to the effect of the golden period. The golden period is unlike anything else that the victim has experienced before (or possibly since, unless they have been ensnared a second time by our kind). It is intense, amazing, scintillating, breath-taking and utterly addictive. Find a thesaurus and pick out any positive emotions and you will experience them all when you are subjected to the blazing glory of the golden period. You will be elated, ecstatic, deliriously happy, excited, overwhelmed with passion and desire, worshipped, adored and placed high, oh so high on a pedestal by us. You will be fully familiar with this golden period and how it felt to you. You know that time period when you felt loved and loved in a way that you had never felt before. This was a perfect love and you returned it to us. You often did not dare to believe how fortunate you were to be on the receiving end of this tsunami of desire but you know what you saw and experienced and of course, seeing is believing isn't it? Whilst all the Casual Actions are effective, the Golden Period is the king. It is this period of time which embeds in you the five Aftermath Effects extensively. You understand what the Golden Period is, but what are the key components of it which generate the Aftermath Effects?

- The provision of the supposedly perfect love which causes you to reciprocate;
- The mirroring of everything which you like and dislike in order to create the impression that you have found your soul mate and your other half;
- The repeated provision of compliments to condition you to expect them and to cause an immediate emotional response in you as a consequence;
- The apparent understanding of your vulnerabilities and weaknesses, the provision of supposed support to tackle those deep-seated injuries;
- Being made to feel ultra-special;
- Seemingly knowing and understanding everything about you so that we "clicked" on every level;
- The creation of the impression that you will never find anybody to rival what we have and thus you wish to maintain this relationship at any and all cost;

- The repeated "future faking" where we promise you a glorious future with us through marriage, commitment, buying a home together, starting a family together and thus providing you with the impression of long-term stability and security;
- The apparent total exposure of ourselves, laying ourselves bare for you in order to cause you to reciprocate;
- The confirmation that true love does exist, something which, as a love devotee, you are committed to;
- Being loved, respected, adored and subjected to a plethora of positive emotions which most human beings want, but often do not attain, only for those emotions to be experienced in the most intense fashion. It is love 2.0.
- The impression that someone knows you inside out and loves everything about you, including your flaws;
- The desire to trust this person with anything and everything, including most precious of all, your heart and soul;
- The creation of many amazing memories and moments together;
- The knowledge that you have finally found "home" and need not look any further. This is the foundation for happiness. The launch pad for a wonderful future together. Dreams can actually come true.

All of these things create a massive imprint on your heart and soul. How does this first Casual Action create the five Aftermath Effects?

a. The golden period is one total illusion;
b. You are supposedly provided with a perfect love and the raw, exposed emotions of another person. You are conned into reciprocating those things whilst being duped into giving your all to equal what you receive, exceed it and keep hold of it. Thus this causes Total Dedication.

c. The realisation that you exposed your own weaknesses, vulnerabilities and that you were taken in by an illusion (which with hindsight appears obvious) causes you to feel like The Fool;

d. You were completely convinced by what we did that you handed your heart to us and allowed us into your soul and into your very being. The wholesale betrayal by us and the absence of truth in anything we ever did for you or said to you shatters your trust and result in The Loss of Trust; and

e. The intensity of the golden period, its addictiveness, the way it was reinforced (compliments again and again, gifts delivered repeatedly, the same amazing love-making, each and every day being wonderful just like the day before) creates The Longing.

Think back to your own Golden Period and identify what made it feel so special to you. It is painful for you to do this because it remains raw (which is entirely what we want) but you will find that what I detailed above will encompass how you felt. It is necessary for you to address and identify the Casual Actions during your golden period so you can see how they resulted in the various Aftermath Effects. This identification is required so you know what it is that needs to be purged.

2. Ever Presence

Ever Presence is a formidable manipulative device which causes you to be reminded of us even when we are not physically proximate. This is a calculated mechanism which we deploy during seduction. One way to look at it is to consider we are like some wild animal marking our territory so that even when we are not there, you are caused to think about us. The existence of Ever Presence is designed so that you activate repeated trip wires each and every day. Those tripwires cause you to think about us and remember us in some context. This will then immediately link you to aspects of the Golden Period again. Those intense emotions associated with the Golden Period come surging to the surface. You may be feeling hurt and upset as you are in the post discard period, but Ever Presence will suddenly cause a burst of bitter sweet happiness, a moment of joy, a period of smiling at those wonderful memories. It is very powerful.

This is a consequence of all the hard work I invested in the Love Bombing technique. In order to overload your senses and sweep you up in my enticing whirlwind of love and affection I did numerous things to ensnare you. I took you to a park and kissed you beneath a spreading oak tree, pushing you gently against the trunk as I whispered in your ear that this was our tree and we would always come back here and kiss beneath its huge boughs. I ensured that several songs became indelibly imprinted in your mind to remind you of you and me being together. I just didn't go for the romantic ones though. No, I ensured that I selected a range of music to accompany every mood and emotion. That upbeat dance track that is associated with our marvellous holiday in Ibiza. That slow waltzing song that we held each other to and listened to on the balcony of my apartment. That frenetic and energetic rock track that we both jumped around to in your living room. You marvelled at how I managed to select certain songs and pieces of music that you loved and seemed so apt for the moment we were caught up in. You did not know that I had already spent time studying the You Tube videos of songs you adore on your Facebook news feed. I have also wheeled out this play list to several other victims and I know it works. I made sure that you would repeatedly see me sat in the same seat in your kitchen reading a Terry Pratchett book. You would then make dinner as I read aloud to you. We always had a bottle of Rioja on a Wednesday evening. I selected four particular restaurants and took you to them repeatedly. I engaged my lieutenants in reinforcing all the wonderful memories associated with dinner parties, trips to the coast and sporting events. Every day there would be a poem left for you under your pillow. I devoured box sets of Breaking Bad, Poldark and West Wing with you. I even learned pieces of the dialogue, which I would repeat from time to time. I specifically wore the same fragrance, used the same anti-perspirant and shower gel so that this created a particular cocktail of scents, which are forever linked to me. My washing powder and fabric conditioner were chosen to stand out for you. Little do you know I have a notebook, which lists each ex-girlfriend and a corresponding list of smells that I used when I was with you. For you it was Chanel Allure Sport, Dove Men and Care Clean deodorant and Molton Brown Black Peppercorn Body Wash. Not that you have forgotten that have you? The dedication by which I ensured I had imprinted myself on your life in every conceivable sense was worthwhile. Not only did I draw you in and ensnare you, but I also left my mark on you so that once I had discarded you (or if you made the bold move of leaving me) I would forever remain with you. You walk through the park and you are haunted by the image of us up against the oak tree. Somebody gets in the lift next to you wearing Chanel Allure and you want to reach out and hug him as you are immediately taken back to smelling me lying next to you in bed. When *With or Without You* is played you start to sob as you recall how I held you close during a thunderstorm as it played in the background (on repeat of course). Everything I did during the Love Bombing was calculated to trap you but was also laying the ground for infecting the afterwards with me. You see me in books, taste me in certain foods and hear my voice when watching a re-run of a programme. You try to escape by avoiding certain things that are poignant reminders, but that means cutting out certain things that you enjoy. Should you make that sacrifice to someone like me? You are torn. Even if you exercise such discipline, I have planted enough reminders around you that you cannot and will not escape me. You go to the newsagents and see The Times newspaper and instantly remember show I would read it on a Sunday as we lounged after making love through the morning. The powerful memory hurts. I am a spectre that follows you everywhere you go. I know this is happening and it gives me a wonderful sense of omnipotent power. I know that I am in your head and heart on a daily basis. I know how much pain this will be causing you. I also know that I still have several hooks deep inside you and it will not take much if I decided to throw a line to you to draw you back in.

The use of Ever Presence is always deployed by us in our engagements with an intimate partner. It is not a happy coincidence that these things happened. You may think it is wonderful and special that we would play certain songs to you in order to convey how much we love you. We did not do this because we loved you. We did this to seduce you and we did it to plant a device that would generate Ever Presence further down the line. I will address this methodology further in this chapter.

How does Ever Presence cause the Aftermath Effects? It does so by causing thought, memory and emotion that is associated with those Aftermath Effects.

a. The existence of Ever Presence will return you in an instant to the Golden Period. If, for example, you hear a particular song it will transport you back to the time we used to dance to that particular song together. You close your eyes and you can see us holding one another and with that image comes the surge of emotion that is associated with what was a wonderful experience. This transportation of you to the Golden Period through Ever Presence causes the effects of the Golden Period to be experienced again with all of the questions that arise from this.

b. Ever Presence will remind you of the Total Dedication you gave to the relationship by reminding you of that relationship and everything that went with it;

c. Ever Presence forms a stark contrast between what you felt during the Golden Period and what you are feeling now. It reminds you of what you fell for, what that felt like and therefore directly rekindles those feelings of being The Fool and the associated questions;

d. Ever Presence returns you to a period when you gave your trust without condition or caveat and once again provides you with a brutal reminder of what you once had had and how that has been stripped from you. Every time you consider how you might rebuild trust, an instance of Ever Presence will remind you of how that trust was abused and cause you to resile from trying to pursue the restoration of trust in order to avoid the consequences of being hurt;

e. Ever Presence always engenders an emotional response. Chief amongst those emotional responses is the desire to return to the Golden Period. You are made to want it again as all those happy memories (which resist being tarnished by what came next) come to the surface and remind you of why the Golden Period was so amazing. You are taken back to it, if only for an instant and you want it back in its totality. You want another chance to make it work and this time ensure that it remains in place. You are still in a position where you may well hold yourself culpable for some or even all of what has happened and therefore (in accordance with this empathic quality) you want the opportunity to make things right once again. You want to try again. This means that the Ever Presence immediately causes your longing and pining again and thus the fifth Aftermath Effect is caused.

3. The Mixture

Whilst Ever Presence operates by reason of taking you back to the place you once thought you would always be, The Mixture functions by making you want to reach out to us once again. The Mixture is implanted inside you as a consequence of the intense nature of the golden period and the seduction which surrounds that. Normal people may find that after the demise of a relationship they will yearn for that person and possibly want to see them again, but the sensation does not last for too long and certainly it does not persist for the duration that is caused by being entangled with our kind. We create in you a desire to want to be with us, to reconnect with us, to establish once again that glorious empire that flourished when the golden period was intact. Such is the strength of this desire it outweighs the knowledge of all the terrible things that we did to you. It is so powerful that it overcomes any reservation about what we are, what we did and how we might behave. It preys on your desire to find perfect love, to heal and to fix. The Mixture is as a direct consequence of how amazing our supposed love was during the golden period. All the while that you were being treated like a queen, all the passion, the tremendous sex, the flattery, the respect, the gifts, the mutual delight in so many topics from film, to books, to holiday resorts, all the friends, all the nights out and trips away, all of these things felt sensational at the time. Part of what was happening was that we were polluting you with The Mixture. Each time we turned to you and smiled as we held hands and walked across than sun-kissed meadow, more drops of The Mixture were fed into you. Every time that we kissed you with undimmed passion and steered you into the bedroom, more mixture was bled into you. Each special word, each delicious act, each "I love you", every bunch of flowers, each whispered compliment, every invitation to dinner, each stroll through the lapping sea meant more and more of The Mixture was leeching into your soul and into your heart. Little by little we fed it to you, you did not know that it was happening but as these toxins permeated your heart and your soul, they coalesced and then sat dormant. This mass has lurked within you for some time. Constructed during the seduction of the golden period and then left to ferment as we devalued you before you either escaped or more likely were discarded, it has sat waiting until such time as you activate it.

Following a normal relationship, it may have ended by mutual consent or one party brought it to an end. Either way there is usually one party who is more upset than another. There follows, in effect, a period of grieving, but it will not last long and thereafter the relevant party moves on with their life. They may occasionally recall happy memories of the relationship from time to time, sometimes triggered in a similar way to Ever Presence but the scale and intensity is far removed from the effect that is caused by us. In a normal relationship, there may be the resurgence of a memory caused by a familiar place or by reason of that person just "popping" into that other person's mind. The memory will last a moment and may evoke a degree of happiness or sadness before drifting away. There it ends.

This is not the case with us. The mixture is activated by two things. The first is Ever Presence, which I have already detailed. The second is triggered by you just happening to think about us. There does not have to be any specific reason why we have entered your head, there may not have been anything which has actually triggered it, but there we are and as soon as we appear the mixture is activated. With that, the mixture immediately causes you to think of something good about us. All of those wonderful things we did during the golden period will be recalled individually (not all at once) by reason of the existence of the mixture. This is a consequence of the imprint we have on your heart and soul. Other people do not touch you in the way we have. We have in effect been branded onto your heart, stitched into your soul and inked indelibly into your mind. Thus when you happen to think about us, you immediately think of something that was good when we were together. That is the mixture activating. You will invariably think of some of the horrible things that we have done to you as your head tries to interfere in the process. Cold brutal logic will be fighting to tell you that we are an awful person, do you not remember all of those terrible things that we did to you? Yes, of course you can, but something else is trying to drown that out. It is the surging emotion as you recall the marvellous things that we did together. You can see me smiling as we spun beneath those oak trees as The Mixture activates. It is easier to given in and allow this image and the associated emotions to flare up inside of you, than to try and fight them. Your head maybe telling you to stop thinking in such glowing terms about us and remember the full horror, but your head (at this stage) is fighting a losing battle with The Mixture. It is stronger, it has hold of your emotions and will allow them to steer you towards remembering the good and the wonderful. The Mixture comes to life and when it does this, it is also relying on our good friend repetition. Every time you think about us in such terms, as driven by The Mixture, you actually make it easier for those thoughts to come again in the future and make it harder to cast them to one side. Imagine wearing a groove in a piece of wood. At first it is hard to make an impression with just one pass of the knife. Do it a second time and there is a little progress. Do it ten times and the groove starts to form. Do it fifty times and the groove goes deeper and each time the knife passes more easily. This is what is caused by The Mixture. It makes you think of us in good terms and each time that you do so, it becomes easier to do it again and again until suddenly you find that your thoughts are becoming dominated by reflecting on what we once had together and you want to reach out to us. You want to find out if there is another chance for you and I, whether there is any possibility of fixing the problems that existed (at this juncture it is unlikely that you have grasped the concept that we cannot be fixed) and whether there is anything that might be done differently this time so that the golden period can be recovered and this time it will stay. The Mixture generates repeated golden thinking about us. This in turn escalates to causing you to want to reach out to us. Perhaps just a text to find out how we are? Maybe you will drive past our house to see if we still live there? You might decide to look around our social media profile and then send us message or post a like on picture to see what response arises. The Mixture causes you to place yourself in our various spheres of influence which then means you will come into our sights again with the inevitable hoover to follow and the risk that the process begins all over again.

The Mixture is insidious and dangerous. It is carefully created when we seduce you and build the golden period. Every magnificent memory and every ecstatic effect causes The Mixture to form inside of you. Eventually, post escape or post discard it will be activated either through Ever Presence invoking a memory or us happening to loom into your thoughts. Once that happens however the Mixture is activated and it soon takes hold of you, gathering pace and strength, overcoming your attempt to apply logic to the situation (much of your logical capability has been disabled or diminished as a consequence of the trauma that you have suffered) and therefore The Mixture prevails. This then will make you reach out to us.

How does The Mixture occasion the Aftermath Effects?

a. The recollection of the good things associated with us provides a link to the Illusion that is the golden period. The feelings and memories will be so real, so intense that you will continue to struggle with the notion that is was actually an illusion;

b. You will be reminded of just how much you gave to us by thinking about us again as a consequence of this being triggered by the Mixture, thus the concept of Total Dedication will remain large in your mind;

c. The Mixture will cause you to recall what was then and what is now and in turn the feelings associated with being fooled will remain;

d. You will be reminded of how much you trusted us and how you wish you could regain that;

e. Every second of every interaction you had with us will be evoked by The Mixture and in turn this will cause you to long for those golden moments once again.

4. Trigger Width

Both Ever Presence and The Mixture rely on triggers. Ever Presence triggers memories and emotions inside of you linked to events and happenings associated with us. The Mixture triggers thoughts about us which build into a desire to reach out to us, similarly linked to those happy memories that you have of us. Although Ever Presence and The Mixture are similar, they are different in the sense that Ever Presence operates by the occasion of external stimuli – seeing a picture of us, smelling a fragrance we would wear. The Mixture is secreted inside of you and can be triggered by your mind just happening to randomly wonder about us. In a way, The Mixture is set on a hair trigger. Since it is always inside of you, waiting for your mind to wander onto something to do with us and then – bang – it is activated. Ever Presence relies on you happening to do something, see, hear or smell something, taste something associated with us for it to be triggered. In order for both of these Casual Actions to be effective we layer them with Trigger Width.

Trigger Width is essentially the mechanism for ensuring that rather than us just have the one chance to trigger Ever Presence or The Mixture, we ensure that there are multiple opportunities. If you fire a gun once at somebody you may hit them, but if you fire it five times or a hundred times you will stand a better chance of striking the target. Furthermore, one bullet on target may kill that target. Two that hit are more likely to do so. Five and the prospects of successfully killing that target improve. It is applying this approach that we want to ensure that we have lots of opportunities for triggers to go off and the more triggers which do go off, the greater the chance that the Aftermath Effects will take place and thus the infection of your heart and soul is more likely to happen. The more trigger events that we can establish, the more extensive the infection will be and the harder it then becomes for you to exorcise the Aftermath Effects from your heart and soul. This in turn means that it is harder for you to move forward. You remain paralysed, unable to free yourself from our grip even though we are no longer with you and as a consequence you remain susceptible to returning to us. This might happen because we decide to hoover you or you may raise your head above the parapet through the effects of the infection and thus draw our attention so that we hoover you.

There must be a significant width or triggers to facilitate our aim. A wide range and a considerable number which are put in place during seduction. Some are placed in order to trigger Ever Presence at a later stage and others are to cause The Mixture to be activated. It is likely to be the case that there will be scores if not hundreds of this triggers put in place by us. The longer the golden period, it stands to reason that there will be more and more triggers that are strewn throughout our involvement. You of course do not know that this is happening. You are too caught up in the wonder and beauty of the golden period but as each precious moment unfolds, as each delicate memory is created and each mesmerising instance occurs, we are laying these triggers all around you. We are creating the link between us and a special moment. We are generating the connection between certain items or moments and particular positive emotions. All through the golden period we are lacing it with the strands that will lead to you in the future so that when you happen to brush against those strands, in the course of an ordinary day by thinking of us or by looking at the window seat where we used to sit reading, you are immediately yanked to the relevant Aftermath Effect or all of them. The more triggers we set out, the more you are likely to set off and the more times each day you will suffer the consequences of the Aftermath Effects. This process also has a further danger for you. Once you trigger a Causal Action, you are likely to trigger another then another and another. Liken it to falling naked into a room with lots of mousetraps. As you put your hand out to get up, you set one off.

You cry out in pain and distracted move your foot which triggers another. You jerk to the side and set off two more along your body and so it goes on. Once you have set off one trigger which leads to an Aftermath Effect, you are more than likely going to set off another.

You see a shirt on someone in a bar which reminds you of us. You then remember the time we wore that shirt when we took you away for the weekend. You remember the repeated trips away that we took together and how I liked to surprise you on a Friday by turning up at work with a suitcase and tickets for you. You remember meeting us for lunch where you worked and sitting in the park nearby as you introduced us proudly to some of your colleagues for this first time as you watched full of admiration as we charmed them pleasantly. Memory knocks into memory which slams into another one, the dominoes toppling over against one another, building up momentum as the emotions begin to climb inside of you and once again you are imbued with the Aftermath Effects of the infection. You cannot believe it was not real, you want us back, you want to experience it again, you know you feel such a fool after what happened and to be taken in after you gave so much, but you cannot trust anybody else, you want us, you want us so, so much and you just want that chance for it to work this time. Sound familiar?

When you are ordinarily trying to negotiate your way through the aftermath of having been entangled with our kind, this trigger width is problematic for you as you can barely move without setting them off. Of course this is entirely deliberate and once you do so, there is a chain reaction and you are deluged by the Aftermath Effects. Now the means to find a way through these triggers and to de-activate many of them exists to you as we shall see in a later chapter.

5. Pervasiveness

We litter the golden period with triggers but we also do this in a pervasive manner. We do not just confine the setting of the triggers to one particular area of your relationship or one particular period of time. The range of these triggers is hugely extensive with the sole intention of ensuring that you are unable to escape setting them off and suffering the Aftermath Effects. For instance, there is little point confining these triggers to say a particular restaurant we went to because if you happened never to go near it again then the trigger will not work and then you will not suffer the Aftermath Effects. You will then be freed from the appearance of the questions, you will not suffer the same emotional responses which paralyse and hold you back. Accordingly, you will be able to move forward and then truly escape our grip by freeing yourself of our infection. No, in order for the Casual Actions to generate the Aftermath Effects we must ensure that the risk of triggering is wide-spread. This is why, during the seduction of the golden period, we will generate links and triggers to every conceivable scenario that involves you and I. Where can you expect these triggers to be placed? They will be placed in the following: -

- Places we visited together
- Restaurants where we dined
- Bars where we drank
- Music and comedy venues we attended
- In music – not just songs that were attributable to our relationship but those songs we sang, for instance, we may choose to sing the same song whenever we were in the shower so if you later hear this you will think of us singing it in the shower once again. We will choose a jingle for an advertisement and sing along to it or add some silly words to make it sound like something else

so that when that jingle plays on the radio or television you will remember us.

- In objects. It might be an umbrella that we always kept by the door, some piece of memorabilia which was rather naff but we never wanted to throw out, an old chair that we had painted and used to sit on. We will imbue various objects with our imprint and then ensure that this object is left behind when we depart from your life so that each time you pick up the expensive kettle we bought or you reach for a book and see our dog-eared copy of *A Tale of Two Cities* you will experience a trigger.

- Food and drink. There will be certain wines we only drink with you, we may have chosen a signature drink which we always ordered in the bar, a vodka martini for example, we may have always cooked meatballs on a Saturday, left crumbs from a fresh loaf we used to pick up on a Sunday. Whatever the food and drink might be will have selected certain items and ensured that, through the repetition and association with us that every time you smell cinnamon you picture us.

- Scents and fragrances. We rely on a sense of smell to convey a very powerful sense of our presence. From washing powder to shower gel, from the cologne we sprayed to the smell of bubble gum in our shampoo, the smell of our car interior because we always bought the same air freshener, that particular smell of polish which we used on our shoes. A catalogue of scents and smells will forever be associated with us.

- We want to place our imprint on your every day. Accordingly, we want you to run the risk of triggers throughout a standard day for you. This means placing those triggers all around the house, from bedroom to bathroom to kitchen, to hallway and outside. On the street, in the car, at the bus stop or the train station. At your work place, at the place where you go for lunch, at your gym, the cinema, the church, the local shops and so on. We will devise a method of causing you to remember us with all of these otherwise routine and mundane places. The time we knocked a stack of cans over in the local convenience store. The fact we always muttered a humorous prayer before entering your parent's house by way of a joke. Each time we got in the car we pretended it would not start.

- Each of your sense will be affected by this. What you smell, taste, see, hear and feel will result in your being reminded of us. Triggers adopt all of the five senses.

- Around the house we will have "our spaces". For instance, we would always watch television from a particular chair, read in a different chair, stand by the fireplace first thing in the evening when we returned from work when we would regale you with our day, sat on one from bottom stair when we waited for you to finish getting ready before going out, the same stool at the breakfast bar, the same chair at the dining table in order to ensure that whenever you look at these places once we have gone you will see our ghost stood there.

- Mannerism, catchphrases and quirks. We may utilise these by reason of association with various tasks. The way we would never walk barefoot on the bathroom floor but always had a trail of towels leading from shower to the bedroom. The fact we always at each item of food on our plate before moving on to the next one and always in an anti-clockwise manner. We might devise certain sayings linked to everyday events, such as saying, "good night Johnboy, good night Mary Ellen" each night as we settled down to sleep or doing a jig if the house telephone rang. Over time and once again through repetition you cannot hear the 'phone ring without picturing our ridiculous jig as we moved to answer it.

It will feel like we have sat down and evaluated all of the things that you do and the places you might go and then we have infected each and every one with our presence. The reality is that we do this as a matter of course throughout the golden period. The greater of our kind will do it more extensively than the lesser and mid-range of our kind, our pervasiveness is more extensive and we will also apply some consideration to what we might do to ensure that we live long in your heart and soul. For the most part however, the creation of this pervasiveness just happens. It is a combination of how we are and also the fact that we manage to imbue even the simplest of actions with something special during the golden period. It as if, through our magnetism and charisma, that we can turn shaking some salt over a meal into an adventure. Everything seems to come alive at our touch, it crackles with energy as we move past it and because of this, the environment is heightened and with it you link it with us. This is also a consequence of your empathic nature as well. You are more receptive to this because of who you are. These markers, signs and triggers are picked up far more readily by you than normal people.

In a way it is akin to walking into a house. Ordinarily normal people would see the walls, the windows, the floors and the furniture. Not you. You can see our imprint all around. It is almost as if we have transferred energy into all of these places which you can sense and see us at the breakfast bar or playing the piano once again. If you run your hand along a benchtop, you can feel that we remain there, where we used to stand singing as we chopped vegetables. This is as a consequence of who you are and furthermore the fact that the connection we fabricated between us was so remarkable and intense that we truly have left our mark on your world and we have done so in such a pervasive manner.

Accordingly, the Aftermath Effects are occasioned by five Causal Actions namely: -

1. The Golden Period (the most powerful of them)
2. Ever Presence
3. The Mixture
4. Trigger Width
5. Pervasiveness

You must be aware of these actions and that **all** of them originate during the seduction. You may think that our seduction of you is the most wonderful thing you have experienced and in many ways it is, but it is also dangerous. It does not seem it but in certain respects it is just as dangerous, if not more so, that the period of devaluation.

Why do we infect you?

It is appropriate to consider why we infect you through the application of Causal Actions to bring about the Aftermath Effects. Those are the methodology, the means by which we execute our infection of you. We take certain steps during seduction so that you suffer the consequences of the Aftermath Effects post-escape or post-discard but why do we do this? What is our strategy? By explaining this you will not only gain clarity of understanding you will now what we are seeking to do to you, so that you can consider this in the actions you need to take to try to counter us and exorcise our infection of your heart and soul.

There are two limbs to our strategy when we infect you. Paralysis and Hoovering

Paralysis

A prime aim is to paralyse you. We may not be physically proximate but we do not want you going anywhere in terms of recovery of emotional progress. We do not want you crossing that metaphorical emotional sea in your liner made of logic and arriving on dry firm land ready to move on with your life. We want you swamped by that emotional sea. I have, in other writing, made reference to the three battles which you face following your discard. The first battle is one which involves emotion and it is worth detailing this battle here to assist your understanding of our thinking.

The first battle following discard is the emotional one. You have been left with no explanation. If one was tendered it made no sense. You cannot reconcile where you are with what has been. The descent from gilded pillar into the dust has been swift and merciless. Every day you have run the gauntlet of scores of emotions, which has drained you, eroded you and taken a significant toll on your well-being. Your emotions are red raw, heightened and easy to trigger. Your pain is extensive, agonising and brutal and it is during this emotional battle that your ally of cool, detached thinking has not fled the battlefield, it never turned up to begin with. Your ability to assess, rationalise and consider you position with the necessary critical analysis evades you. All you are left with is a cauldron of emotion, which serves only to heighten your distress and your confusion. Nothing makes sense and you have not been left in a position to make any sense of what has happened. This is entirely deliberate. I know so many of you use the phrase "hot mess". This is entirely apt. You are a mess. Your life is a mess. The heat comes from your raging emotions as you veer between hysteria and anger.

Of the three battles that you fight post discard, the emotional battle, the first, is the one which you invariably end up losing. This is because you are utterly ill-equipped. If you were an army your troops would be sharing guns, you would not know which way to face, your supply lines have been overstretched and in some places broken and the enemy seems to appear at will. The fog of war obscures your vision. Is that us advancing or just the silhouette of a tree? You cannot tell. Once you could, but no longer. It is a tortuous place and one which has been created through our design in order to ensure that when return (and we will) you will be in no position to resist. Weakened, governed by emotion rather than intellect you will be overrun easily. This is when the hoover operates. This battle, where all you have is emotion, means that you want the pain to stop. You want the golden period again. You give no consideration or thought to what might be the price of such desires, or whether it really is the golden period once more. You are ruled by emotion and this proves to be your downfall. We know this and this is why we ensure you are a churning, broiling scorching crucible of emotion. We create it, we want that. This is why your first attempt at no contact (without the benefit of specialist input) nearly always falls. You are not equipped to prolong it because in this emotional battle all it takes is for us to come galloping over the hill once again, offering terms of the golden period and you surrender in an instant allowing us to occupy your territory once more in the understandable but ultimately forlorn hope of a peaceful co-existence.

How do you win this emotional battle? You cannot. You are in such a position that we always win this battle. The key however is not to participate in this battle but rather avoid it altogether. If you know there is a battle you cannot win, why would you ever fight it? You would not. You would evade your foe, take steps to bolster your defences and seek to avoid this emotional battle. This is what you must do. Once you have gained awareness of the foe you are engaged with, possibly during seduction or more likely through the period of devaluation, you must then take those steps to prepare yourself. You either avoid the emotional battle altogether by escaping rather than being discarded. Alternatively, you steel yourself for the inevitable discard so that the emotional fallout is massively reduced and instead you find yourself transported to the second battle that takes places post discard which I shall expand on in a further article.

If you have been discarded, then you face the emotional battle and you will lose. You must avoid the emotional battle in its entirety or engage on terms in the second battle which follows post discard.

Since you are unable to win this emotional battle we want to keep you fighting in and therefore this is why part of our strategy is to paralyse you. We do not want you to make sense of what has happened to you. We do not want you trying to apply cold logic to your situation (which is what happens in the second post discard battle) because if you do there will come a time (even though you may have to find this second battle a dozen or more times) when you will emerge from the first two battles and ready to engage in the third which is where you are in a much stronger position.

We want you in the weakened position and stuck in this emotional turmoil. If we can achieve this, you will never move forward and you will never escape us. Yes, you may not be physically with us but you will remain in our grip and this imbues us with a great sense of omnipotence. By keeping you in one place, we then know that you are weakened, governed by emotional responses, primed to give us more fuel when we so choose and you cannot see a way out. We do not want you re-connecting with those people we isolated you from when we seduced and devalued you. Those people may provide you with additional insight, support and encouragement which will work against us. That must not happen. We want to know that we have dealt you a crippling blow so you cannot escape us and you will always be stuck in the same place ready for our return which leads us to the second limb of our strategy.

The Potential to Hoover

Whether you have escaped us or whether we discarded you, rest assured there will be a hoover at some point. Many people struggle to grasp the idea that we will not ever leave them alone. I often think the word "discard" is mis-leading since this suggests some kind of finality. I think the word "dis-engage" would be more appropriate, since this is what we do. We temporarily put you to one side but we do not truly let go of you. Not at all. That is the whole point of infecting your heart and soul, why we deploy the Causal Actions and want to bring about the Aftermath Effects. We do all of this so that you are paralysed and then we know that we can waltz back in and hoover you with ease because you remain vulnerable and susceptible to us doing so.

It is not a question of whether we will hoover you but rather when. It is governed by a number of factors but the most relevant one is the question of whether you appear in our spheres of influence. It is therefore worth explaining what those spheres are.

There are numerous factors which govern whether we will attempt to hoover you post-escape or post-discard. Some of these factors determine the style of the hoover, whether it will be malign or benign and also how often the attempts will be made. There are several considerations which have a material impact on whether a hoover will occur and one of the most significant ones is the sphere of influence and your relationship to it.

Imagine if you will, me. Now I know you do this often as your guilty little secret but we haven't got time for that at the moment. Here I am sat at home, or in the office, or walking between bars. Let us take an instance of me being in a bar. What is my sphere of influence? To be accurate there are actually several. They vary in applicability and range. The first is the physically proximate sphere, namely those who are within earshot. That is the closest sphere of influence and unsurprisingly the most dangerous for you. It is within this sphere of influence when the full range of charismatic and magnetic charms can be deployed in order to pull you back into my influence. Anybody who I can speak to or listen to, be sat with, or dine with, stand next to or be near is in this sphere of influence.

The second sphere is the eye line sphere. This is the sphere where I can see you or you can see me. We may be across the street, on the other side of a field, up in an office, walking across a plaza, across from you on the piste. If we can see you or you can see us, then you are in this sphere. I may not be able to communicate with you other than to shout or wave but it remains a sphere of influence. Accordingly, this is why when we seek to hoover somebody we may not be able to speak directly with them but we can position ourselves stood across from your house on the other side of the street or waiting across the square from where you leave work.

The third sphere of influence is our reach through our coterie and our lieutenants. Whether these people are our friends (inner or outer circle), colleagues, minions or family, if they operate as our lieutenants or our coterie they form part of a sphere of influence. If you speak to these people (therefore operate in their first sphere) or they see you or you see them (therefore in the second sphere) you are caught within my third sphere of influence. Rest assured that news of your appearance in the spheres of my lieutenants and my coterie will be relayed to me. This may be in person, by telephone, text or e-mail message, but the news will reach me. This also allows me to send information to you by proxy as my coterie and lieutenants tells you about what I am doing, who I am with and so on and so forth.

The fourth sphere of influence is our reach through the telephone. I do not mean by text messages or FB messenger but actually speaking on the telephone. Whilst we may be thousands of miles from you, unseen and not physically proximate at all, the fact you are speaking to us allows us to extend our reach in an effective way through the use of the telephone. Facetime and Skype and similar applications fall within this sphere as well.

Next there is the fifth sphere of influence which manifests through the sending of text messages, e-mails, letters, notes wrapped around bricks thrown through your window, smoke signals etc. There is no actual speaking to one another. There is no third party involved. There is no physical proximity. This is the fifth sphere.

Finally, there is the sixth sphere of influence which is my mind. You may pop up in my mind for no reason whatsoever. It might be I hear a song which reminds me of you or I walk past where you used to live and I reminded of you. In all other respects I have deleted you from my mind post discard or post escape but then something happens, either triggered by something or just a random recall and there you are, in my mind and in my thoughts and therefore you have entered the sixth sphere of influence.

Following your escape or your discard we will operate all five of these spheres in an attempt to hoover you. Once you appear in any or all of these spheres of influence this will encourage us to effect a hoover (bearing in mind other factors as well which I will detail on a separate occasion). Thus if you have been effecting no contact and then I see you on a bus travelling along the high street, you have entered my second sphere of influence. You have come to my attention. You are on my radar. This may cause me to wave at you and get your attention or run along the road to catch up with the bus and board it so I can bring you into my first sphere. I may be minded then to make efforts to contact you in some other fashion, but the fact you have sailed close to me, appeared in my sphere does two things.

One, it alerts me to you. I may have been distracted with other sources of fuel but you entering my sphere of influence makes you game for a hoover.

Two, it awakens the mixture in you, that addictive quality that we imbue in you through our nefarious seduction of you, which then causes various memories to awaken inside of you, thoughts and feelings which make you vulnerable to our overtures once again.

Thus we will then look to hoover you. We are reminded of you and this calls into mind the potent hoover fuel that is on offer. Secondly you are at a heightened risk of the hoover succeeding because of the effects of the mixture that lurks inside of you, place there by us some time ago when we seduced you.

Sometimes we seek to draw you into our sphere of influence. If we wait around outside where we know you work, we are trying to draw you into our sphere of influence. More often however it is you that enters our sphere of influence, either deliberately or inadvertently.

For example, you may decide you need to return some of our property and you call round to drop it off. You have entered our first sphere of influence through this act and you will be hoovered. Alternatively, it is late at night and we are on your mind (but you are not on ours) and you cannot help but send a text asking us how we are doing. By doing this you have entered our fifth sphere of influence. Any step or act which brings you to our attention, whether in person, on the 'phone, through others or through technology is you entering our sphere of influence and triggering a likely hoover.

There remains a risk of a hoover (that is why we never truly go away) because of this sixth sphere of influence, but the risk is reduced if you are able to stay out of the first five spheres of influence. Naturally we want you blundering into them and the infection you suffer is designed to bring that about. The consequence of the

Aftermath Effects will have you struggle to keep out of one or more of the spheres of influence. You are therefore on our radar. Furthermore, because of the paralysis that our infection has caused your defences will be weakened and the hoover that we deploy in order to draw you back into our world will more than likely succeed.

Accordingly, the outcome of the infection and the Causal Actions and their Aftermath Effects is to paralyse you, make you enter one or more of our spheres of influence so we are alerted to you again and thus the inevitable hoover that follows will succeed because you are unable to defend against it.

We then draw fuel from you, delicious, potent hoover fuel and we have hauled you back into our grip once again and so the cycle is able to start again. That is the ultimate aim of our infection and that is why it is so important for you to exorcise this infection of your heart and soul because if you do not do so you remain highly vulnerable to the narcissistic cycle happening to you again and again and again.

Why is it especially effective?

As part of increasing your understanding of how we use this infection of your heart and soul before you carry out the exorcism, it is worthwhile briefly considering why this infection is so effective. What you have read so far will leave you in no doubt as to how powerful the effects of our machinations are in causing this infection and indeed you may well have felt those effects and thus you can testify as to their impact on you. There are also a handful of additional considerations you should have regard to which explain why this infection is especially effective.

1. You were selected as our victim for several reasons but one of those reasons includes the fact that you are an emotional individual. This impacts on many areas of our entanglement but it means that you are more vulnerable that a normal person to the effects of our infection. You give a heightened response and the impact is more severe and long-lasting. You need to understand that this is the case as it is applicable to how you conduct the exorcism in that particular chapter.

2. You are placed in a position of vulnerability when the infection is commenced. You might think that you are strong when the seduction takes place but the reality is that you are not. The fact you are vulnerable to being seduced by our kind also means that you will be vulnerable to the infection.

3. You have exposed your heart and soul to us as a consequence of the method of our seduction. If you had not done this, we would not have been able to have infected you. You need to allow us access to your heart and soul, without restraint, condition of caveat. By doing this you have stripped away any defences that might exist, any obstacles which might affect the

effectiveness of the infection and allowed us a prime shot. The risk of the infection of your heart and soul failing is thus minimal, if not negligible.

4. The repetitive nature of what we do increases the effectiveness of infection.

5. The layering of different methodologies to achieve the infection and its effects increases the prospects of success.

6. Your empathic traits – your belief in love, your honesty, decency and you high level of trust (along with many others) means that you are at a heightened risk of infection and thus the methods we use are far more effective. In the same way that an elderly person has a reduced immune system and therefore is at a greater risk of disease, the existence of your empathic traits makes you at greater risk of our infection.

7. The fact that when we have discarded you (and also even when you escape us) you will be grieving in some form for what you once had. This form of grieving is especially important because you may think that you are grieving the loss of the person that you adored and loved beyond anything else. You are not actually grieving for the loss of us. This is because you never knew us. We did not allow you to know who we really are. That was never shown to you. What makes the infection hugely effective is the fact that you are actually grieving for yourself. It is generally accepted that when you are seeking an intimate partner you are looking for someone who is similar to yourself, in effect your other half which completes you. This is why people make reference in a colloquial way to their "other half". You are looking for someone who is the other half of you. Therefore, you want someone who shares your interests, your values, your morals and your outlook on life. You want someone who likes similar music to you, enjoys the same type of films, books and entertainment as you. If you do not like ballet, you do not want someone who is a regular attender. If you dislike guns, you do not want an active member of a rifle club. Naturally, one does not invariably find a perfect fit for all these likes and dislikes and you hope to have as many

"hits" or "ticked boxes" as possible. Of course, when we come along we just happen to tick more boxes than anybody else and you think we are the perfect intimate partner. This is because all we have done is mirror you and caused you to fall in love with yourself. This is why the connection with us seems so powerful and strong because we have given you (under false pretences) the very thing that you want more than anything; yourself.

Accordingly, when the relationship has ended you are left grieving for that supposedly perfect love which in actual fact leaves you grieving for yourself. That is why it strikes you to the core, hurts you so much and takes such a long time to recover from (if you ever can fully recover from this). The fact that we cause you to fall, effectively, in love with yourself and leave you with such grieving for yourself thereafter is another reason why the effectiveness of our infection is so great.

Resting Point

Before we turn to the various techniques that you can deploy to exorcise us from your heart and soul, it is worth pausing a moment to reflect on where you have got to.

It is important for you to ascertain which stage you are at in respect of your entanglement with your narcissist so you can ascertain the degree to which the infection has commenced and thereafter gauge the applicability of the exorcism.

You now know the five Aftermath Effects that have to be exorcised. That is crucial. Hitherto, you may have declared: -

"I just want him out of my heart."

"I want to stop feeling like this."

"I just want to stop thinking this way."

Such sentiments are entirely understandable but they do not specify what it is that you are trying to purge. If you do not truly understand what it is you are trying to get rid of it, how then can you actually do so? You have gained understanding and insight into what the Aftermath Effects of the infection are. You also now know what it is what we do to bring about those Aftermath Effects through the application of our Causal Actions. You know how we achieve the potency of this infection, the methods deployed and when they are deployed, all of which assist your understanding. As I have written many times, the more you understand, the easier it becomes. This is not just because you are finally gaining comprehension but it means that you are diminishing the emotional effects of our entanglement and instead trying to remain within the boundaries of applying logic and intelligence. We do not want you doing this because it weakens our grip. We thrive on keeping you emotional. We want you stuck, as I wrote above, in the emotional turmoil following the end of the relationship. We do not even want you to engage in the battle that follows, the one between heart and head because there is a chance, albeit slim at first but it increases the more you fight the battle, that you will begin to pull clear of the emotion and in turn distance yourself from our toxic influence.

It is worth considering what goes on in this second battle because when you apply the techniques in the next chapter, you are engaged in the battle of heart versus head. We want to use your emotions against you. You need to apply rational though and logic to steer a course through the emotion and bring about a successful exorcism

The first battle that takes places post discard is the Emotional Battle. That is a battle that you are always destined to lose. You will always fight at least one Emotional Battle because you do not know any other way. In all likelihood, you will face several of these post discard battles because you will keep being hoovered back into our grasp until such time as you learn to recognise what you are dealing with and understand what you must do. Eventually and this may take several Emotional Battles before you realise this and are capable of achieving the appropriate response, you either evade the Emotional Battle by escaping as opposed to being discarded, or you prepare yourself for the eventual discard in a manner which means you no longer have to ensure the Emotional Battle. Instead, you move on to the next post discard battle, that of Head versus Heart ("the HvH Battle").

The HvH Battle (also known as the Logic v Emotion Battle) is a battleground where you stand some chance of victory. This battleground is one where you have gained understanding. It might be through your repeated exposure to our kind so that eventually something has "clicked" into place or more often than not it is as a consequence of an external agent who has explained matters to you. It might by a therapist, a friend, the content of a book, something you saw on YouTube or even something that I have written. Whatever has caused this understanding to increase, it is this which provides you with the fighting chance to win this HvH Battle.

You have been discarded and run the gamut of emotional fall-out thereafter. You may understand what we are. You may understand some of the things that we have done. You may be familiar with the fact that we will try to hoover you back into our grip. You may even be starting to comprehend that what has happened was all predicated on an illusion. The degree of understanding will vary but what is important for you is that you are allowing logical thought to be heard above the raw heat of your emotions. You once again will not just be battling against us but also yourself. We will be looking to hoover you in order to draw you back into our grip or perhaps we will be unleashing a malign hoover since we are unable to draw you back into our false reality and therefore we opt to keep extracting negative fuel by way of punishment for your treachery. You have us as an opponent, but you will also be fighting yourself as your emerging logic grapples with the still churning emotion. You have learned many things and you know you should apply what you have learned but still there is the emotional pull that you experience. You are not removed or detached from your emotions, they have not dimmed either, they are still there, raging away. The hurt, the love, the longing, the passion, the fear and the upset. An ocean of emotion which you once tried to cross but that was the Emotional Battle and you had barely taken four strokes as you began to swim before you were engulfed by the emotion and sank to the bottom of this sea, drowned by your own emotion. Now you have built a vessel. It is made from cool, hard logic. Critical thinking, once a stranger to you during your savage devaluation, has re-appeared. You can analyse and assess. It is unlikely you are able to do so at the level you once enjoyed before we came along but it is there. Whether this vessel is a tiny raft, a dinghy, a boat or a hulking great liner depends very much on the extent of your understanding. The choppy emotional seas will smash against your vessel of logic. A wave of sorrow will buffet you, a tsunami of longing will threaten to swamp you once again. Wave after wave of emotion will try and capsize your vessel as you try to navigate this emotional ocean. Chances are your life raft will be smashed to match wood and you will be tipped into the sea to drown once again as emotion subsumes you and you find yourself back in our hold. Your clipper may be holed beneath the waterline and you start to take on board more and more emotion as steadily you sink beneath the emotional waves once again. It is during this HvH Battle as you try to cross the emotional ocean, because what you must do is reach the dry land beyond and in effect put an ocean but you and us, you will be subjected to the push and pull of your emotions trying to guide you, to control your decision-making, your head will tell you one thing as your heart screams something else at you. This is probably the harder battle for you to fight. In the Emotional Battle, you do not stand a chance and your defeat is swift and total. During the HvH Battle you will make gains, suffer losses, seem to making a breakthrough and then out of nowhere a tidal wave will flip you from your boat and into the churning ocean and you drown once again. All the while we will be whipping up the waves, firing our torpedoes at you as we endeavour to cause you to sink into this emotional ocean yet again and you fail to cross it and win this battle. How might this HvH Battle manifest in the real world?

1. You will know you ought not to contact us but you need to send a message to see if we respond.
2. You will keep checking our social media profiles to ascertain if you are mentioned, if we are with somebody else and/or to find out what we are doing.
3. You will ask about us to our coterie and lieutenants, often unwittingly doing so, so this is fed back to us.
4. You will go on dates but find you are always comparing this new person to us and they are always found to be wanting.

5. You know what the outcome will be but you just want one more night with us.

6. You realise that we are unlikely to change but if you do not try you will ever know, so it is worth one more attempt to talk isn't it?

7. You understand much of what we did and said was a lie, but surely it could not all have been an illusion? There must have been times where we really did love you and you need to ask us about this.

8. You know we are bad for you, but you cannot help what you feel. Surely it would be better to stop this pain from being there all the time and just have it occasionally?

9. You know you should not reply to our messages but it feels so good to have a conversation with us again. It has been too long.

10. You know we are using you, but it feels so damn good.

11. One kiss cannot hurt can it?

12. You know better now, so going back will be different because you know what to expect. Armed with this new knowledge you can enter the lion's den again but be better prepared.

13. You know we are bad for you but you cannot bear the thought of someone else being with us and perhaps being the one to work.

14. What if this time the apology is sincere and the desire to change is real? If you walked away from that, you would only be denying yourself happiness wouldn't you?

15. You understand engaging with us is dangerous but there are things you really need to tell us.

These and others besides are all examples of the inherent tension that arises in this tug-of-war between your cool intellect and your burning emotions.

Can you win this battle that rages post discard? Unlike the first battle, the Emotional Battle which you can never win, you can be victorious. You may have to fight this HvH Battle many times before securing the win. In the beginning you may be clinging to little more than a log as you desperately try to sail the emotional ocean and you are swept from it. However, by reading and understanding, by disciplining yourself to apply logic, to prevent your emotions from engulfing you, by reading more and increasing your knowledge you will begin to increase your logic vessel. From log to raft to dinghy. Still you may be swamped and drowned again. But then it becomes a small boat, a yacht, a clipper, a steamer, a passenger liner, a frigate, a destroyer and a super tanker. Each time you rebuild, better, bigger and stronger as you learn more, making the vessel more seaworthy. You begin to chart routes so you avoid the most tumultuous emotional areas, finally beginning to steer through calmer waters until there it is, on the horizon, the sight of land and the final battle that occurs with our kind post discard.

The HvH Battle is not an easy battle. You will fight it several times, but each time you should be better prepared to cross the emotional ocean and improve your prospects of success. Sometimes you are taken unawares by some of our provocative tactics and dumped unceremoniously into the water once again, but it is a battle you can win through the dedicated application of knowledge and understanding.

Accordingly, it is not only just a case of knowing how you can perform this exorcism but it is also knowing why it must be done because understanding that increases your prospects of success and increases your defences.

You have also understood why the infection is especially effective and the factors behind this.

Thus, you stand on the brink of performing your exorcism to drive our infection from your heart and soul. You are ready to do this in the context of the second post discard battle as you apply this knowledge (head) and we fight to keep you where we want you (heart). Not only will this understanding assist you whilst performing this exorcism for the reasons outlined you should now be in a position to take away something absolutely crucial. This understanding should now have you realising something fundamental that we will also maximise your prospects of successfully implementing the exorcism.

The infection was not your fault. Not one single part of it. You, although we want you to think to the contrary, are blameless.

Keep hold of that thought. You will need it for what comes next.

The Exorcism

Armed with your increased understanding which you can only gain from having it explained to you by our kind, you are now in the best possible place to perform your exorcism and in so doing purge us from your heart and soul. The various techniques that follow are written again from our perspective so you can gain understanding and encouragement as to why these techniques are so effective, rather than the blind hope that they will work because this is what someone has told you. I know from those that have done similar (albeit not on the same scale nor with the same degree of understanding that I have provided here) that these methods are successful in driving us from within you, but in those instances those successes were only partial. This book and these techniques below are designed so that your exorcism achieves totality and you will rid us from your heart and you will purge us from your soul.

The Shift in Thinking

There are actually three constituent parts to achieving the shift in thinking.

(1)   From the Emotional to the Rational

We start with this technique because you have actually commenced this already by reading this book. You have shifted (or begun to shift) your thinking away from being mired in emotion and confusion, to instead moving to gaining an understanding. This step in itself is important for the reasons which I have explained above. If you remain thinking in an emotional state, you will not do so with any clarity, you will make bad decisions, you will be trying to engage us on the very battleground which suits us best. By shifting your thinking away from the emotional to one of logical understanding, you are reducing the effect of the damage that we cause. You are lessening the hold that we have on you. You are managing to haul yourself out of the swamp which threatened to drag you under and keep you in one place. Thus, this immediate shift in thinking is a beneficial step to achieving the purge.

(2)   Reject the Memory

It is not just this movement from emotional thinking to logical thinking that helps you but also a shift in your thinking in itself, namely the way that you think. I referred above to the image of falling naked into a room full of mousetraps and how you set one off, then another and another. When you succumb to Ever Presence you allow the memory to wash over you. This is understandable because it will evoke pleasant feelings which contrast with the pain and misery that you are enduring post-discard. You want a break from the agony and allowing those wonderful memories to take hold again gives you that respite. Of course, it is a slippery slope because if you allow the memory to take hold, you will then drift into another one, then another as like dominoes they clatter into one another, more and more tumbling as you take that trip back down memory lane. They gather momentum and it becomes harder and harder to stop thinking about them and also to resist the effects of such recollections. You find the longing is even greater now and you desperately want to connect with us and thus that text is sent and you appear in our sphere of influence. You are vulnerable to the hoover and it succeeds and you are back in the grip of the narcissistic cycle once more.

You need to discipline your thought process. This takes time and effort but with anything, the more you do it, the easier it becomes. Should a memory or thought of us manifest, cast it aside immediately. Initially, you are not able to prevent the memory arising (we will look at that later) so what you must do is not allow it to linger. Accept that in the initial days and weeks following discard we will keep "popping" into your mind. Do not expect to screen us out from the very outset. That just will not happen and if you believe that that can happen you are setting yourself up to fail and you will not persevere with your exorcism. Understand the thought will come and the memory will arise and when it does immediately cast it aside. Do not allow it to consume you, do not embrace it, do not give it life. As soon as any thought or memory concerning us first blooms in your mind, throw it out. The more you do this, the more it becomes an almost automatic response as you train your mind to reject us. You are not allowing that groove to be made in your mind so that it easy to keep thinking about us.

Now, it may sound easy enough to just cast the thought aside as soon as it forms, but you are hampered because there is an emotional response that accompanies it and this is what tries to pin you down to keep thinking the thought or wallowing in the memory. The key to causing a shift in your thinking is to cause a shift in your doing. If you remain doing the same thing, then you are giving the thought or memory more of a chance to hang around. You need to harness the power of a quick distraction. Accordingly, if the thought or memory arises in the following scenarios then apply shift in doing to cause your shift in thinking.

Situation	Action
Watching television	Move to the kitchen and make a drink
Waiting for food to cook	Telephone a friend
Sat in car whilst driving	Turn on radio for music or talk
Whilst showering	Start singing
Walking down street	Telephone a friend or listen to music
Reading a book	Tidy up
At your desk at work	Leave your office or workspace and talk To someone else
Whilst shopping	Buy the next blue or green item you see

Those are just suggestions, the key is to do something immediate and different. You need to train your mind so that as soon as the memory or thought about us begins you stop what you are doing and do something else instead. That "jolt" will distract you and allow you to throw the thought about us out of your mind. If the thought persists, change tack again. Although it is not always possible, the best change of tack is to engage with somebody because then you will focus on what this person is saying and doing and what you are saying and doing with them.

You need to discipline yourself to know that: -

1. Allowing the memory to linger is forbidden;
2. The memory is to be cast out;

3. The easiest way to do this is to seek a distraction;
4. The fastest way to find a distraction is to stop what you are doing and do something else;
5. The best distraction is another person (if possible).

Over time not only will you be caused to think about us less (see below) but when you do so, your shift in thinking will be an automatic defence so you will not want to linger with the memory but you will do something alternative and in turn dispel the thought. It takes practice and it takes discipline but you will achieve it over time.

(3)   The New Reality

The third part of altering your shift in thinking is to comprehend what has actually happened to you and what you were actually dealing with. You need to keep reminding yourself of what really happened and accept that. This will prevent you from engaging in the various questions concerning "what if" and will also assist you in banishing all of the questions that come with the Aftermath Effects which I described above.

Central to accepting the new reality is the need to accept the following.

We did not love you.

The golden period was an illusion.

Nothing was your fault.

We cannot be fixed.

Everything we did was fake.

You did not know us.

You will try to reject these concepts because it hurts to much and because the Aftermath Effects are designed to cause you to challenge these ideas by making you think, "He must have loved something about me, nobody would behave like that."

The answer to that is.

"He did not love you. Yes, we do behave like that."

Every time you find yourself challenging and questioning these points of the new reality you must learn to reject the challenge. In a similar way to rejecting the thought or memory of us, you must not accept the challenge to the new reality. If you find yourself thinking,

"Surely with enough love, he could change his ways?"

You need to tell yourself.

"I did nothing wrong. All my love would not change him. He cannot be changed." Then seek a quick distraction.

We want you unsure and challenging this reality. We want you to be unable to accept that someone could behave in such an extraordinary way but they can because you have just experienced it.

The key to reinforcing this new reality and ensuring you do not challenge it is to read and to understand. Happily, you have access to many of my books which will increase and improve your understanding so more and more you accept that we did not love you. Over time, you will challenge less and less until, as the emotion recedes as well, should we ever pop into your mind you will straight away think.

"He was a fraud. He did not love me."

There will be no doubt. There will be no reflection or rumination on whether this is right or not and you will feel considerably better.

Part of preventing you from moving on is what I call the Wrong Focus. This is the consequence of the Aftermath Effects and which I mentioned above. You can smash the Wrong Focus by understanding the answers to those questions which form part of the Wrong Focus. Happily, for you, I am going to provide you with those answers now, so that if you find yourself asking the question you will know the answer straight away by reading it here. That is the definitive answer because one of our kind has given you it, nobody else and nobody is going to know better than one of our kind, with my awareness. Here are the answers.

1. You will wonder why we treated you so terribly after we were so wonderful to you.
   We did this because you stopped providing us with potent positive fuel. We needed to draw negative fuel from you instead in order to maintain our existence.

2. You will want to know how we could have just left you like that after everything that you did for us?
   With absolute ease. We only think of ourselves. You are just an appliance to us not a person. Someone else has our interest now and we regard them as better than you on every front.

3. You will be perplexed as to how we are able to move on to somebody else so soon after being with you, especially since we said that you and I were soulmates and would be together until the end of time?
   Those are standard hook-lines (look out for a forthcoming post on this) which we scatter like confetti in order to seduce them. We rarely mean anything we say to you as we are habitual liars

4. What are we doing with our new acquisition?

   More or less exactly what we did with you. Seducing them and giving them the golden period. We will apply similar techniques to how we charm and mesmerise them as we did with you. Expect us to say the same things, take them to the same places, buy the same gifts and so on, with some occasional changes.

5. How are they better than you?

   How long have you got? They are more beautiful, more loving, more intelligent, more successful, more fun, more admiring, more adoring, in fact whatever you were they are a thousand times better.

   The truth is they are not, they may even be less than you, but we do not see that. To us they are shiny and new and thus amazing.

6. Are we happy with that person now?

   We don't feel happy. We feel engorged by the power that surges through us from the fuel. We tell everyone we are happy though in order to maintain appearances and also in the hope you hear about our huge joy with this person.

7. What has that person got that you haven't?

   To us, the most wonderful and potent positive fuel.

   In your reality, they are little different, indeed you would be surprised by just how much in common you would have.

8. She doesn't even seem like our type so why on earth have we chosen her?

   If she pours out positive fuel she is our type. That is all that matters. You are all appliances in our eyes.

9. You spend your time on "Ex Watch" as you stalk our social media (and that of the new target) to see what we are doing together, what we are saying to one another and looking for any signs of trouble in this new relationship. We want you doing this so you will not move on. You will not see any signs of trouble in paradise. Quite the contrary as we pump out the propaganda.

10. You want our new relationship to fail so you feel better and validated because the same thing has happened to the new target as it did to you. We know you do because that is how hateful and horrible you are and makes us wonder why on earth we ever chose. Don't worry though, it will eventually falter, they always do.

11. You feel a need to prove that you are happy (even though you are not) and that you need us to know that this is the case. You consider ways in which you can convey this message to us.
Don't bother. We know you are torn apart and we will just laugh at your attempts to pretend otherwise. We can still sense what is really going on. Instead of appearing happy you would do better to appear neutral and unmoved.

12. You wonder what you could do to win us back.
You really shouldn't bother but you don't have to do anything because we will hoover you soon enough.

13. You wonder what mistakes were made that caused the relationship to fall apart.
How long have you got for us to list your litany of transgressions? The fact is that this is the case from our perspective. You did nothing wrong.

14. You begin to imagine what is going on in between those four walls, that you knew so well once upon a time, becoming fixated with considering what is happening.

Everything that happened between you and I. It is actually frightening just how similar it is.

15. You relive the day you had with us and think about whether we are doing the same things with the new person as we did with you.

Of course we are.

16. You want us to explain why we did what we did?

Not going to happen. We need to keep you hanging on for answers and closure.

17. You try to make sense of what has happened but you cannot. This does not, however, stop you from running the whole relationship through your head over and over again as you seek to find answers.

There is no point doing this. The answer does not lie there.

18. You sit and ask yourself are we thinking about you?

No we aren't. You don't exist to us until you appear in a sphere of influence and then it is hoovering time.

19. You ruminate on whether we miss you at all.

We don't miss you at all. We might miss your fuel at some point.

20. Does she kiss us like you did?

Yes, not that we care.

21. Do we love her more than we loved you?

    We will tell the world and you (and her) that we have never loved anyone like this before. Of course we have. It is always the same even though it is not love as you understand it.

22. Have we kept the gifts you gave us?

    Yes. They will be used to hoover and triangulate.

23. Why have we deleted all the pictures of you on social media?

    To provoke you and keep the new target happy.

24. Why haven't we deleted all the pictures of you on social media?

    To provoke you and keep you hanging on.

25. Why are we saying those things about you to other people?

    It's a smear campaign, get used to it. Everybody gets them. You are nothing special.

26. Do we feel bad at the way that we treated you?

    No.

27. Why does it feel like no matter what you do we always seem to win?

    Because we change the rules to suit us.

28. Will we ever speak to you again?

    Oh yes. When it is hoovering time.

29. Will our friends and family still acknowledge you after everything that has happened?

No. The smear campaign is in effect. They will when we hoover you though.

30. What if she is "the one"?

Of course she is. The replacement is always the one (until the next one).

Applying this shift in thinking will be hard because of the way the infection has been created but the more you do it, the quicker it will protect you and the easier it will become to do it. All of these techniques mesh together to become greater than the sum of their parts.

Deletion

You need to delete us from your life. There are four fundamental points to consider when applying deletion as part of the exorcism.

(1) Undertaking this will hugely reduce the instances of Ever Presence;

(2) You will feel a sense of relief and progress once you have done this;

(3) Get even. Understand that when we discarded you, we deleted you from our life. To us you never existed as we became fixated with your replacement. Yes, you will exist again if you enter a sphere of influence, but right now, you have been deleted. Do the same to us.

(4) We hate two things more than anything. Being criticised and being ignored (which in itself is a criticism). By deleting us you are ignoring us in a massive way and not only will this play a huge part in your exorcism of us, it will wound us too.

This deletion needs to be ruthless and without mercy. There is no room for sentiment. All and any reminders of us, connections to us and links to us must be removed without qualification or caveat. I recommend you enlist the assistance of a trusted supporter to aid you with this task because you may waver and not perform this exercise with the total ruthlessness that is necessary. If you think books about decluttering your life and your home were ruthless, think again. You should set aside appropriate time for this deletion. Do it over a weekend or take a couple of days off work and organise a reward for yourself (and your loyal supporter) after the process has been completed. You need time to do it correctly. You need to allow time also because you will be tested as you will be confronting repeated reminders and this will be upsetting for you but there is no other way to do this and the sooner you undertake it the better.

Remember, we are relying on the following: -

- You not wanting to do this because you are mired in emotion;
- You wallow in sentimentality;
- You feel "bad" for removing things we got for you during the golden period;
- You will do it half-heartedly;
- You will make excuses for keeping things;
- You will give up

We know you are at risk of these factors and indeed we rely on them. I am telling you that we know these are the things which will hinder you and therefore you need to gird your loins and show us that you can do it. This is why it is important to have a true supporter to hand to drive you through this painful process.

Ensure you have plenty of boxes, bin bags and such like and do not place the items into storage in and around your house. What you are about to delete has to go, not be placed in a holding pen somewhere which you might come across in six months.

You should perform this deletion with regard to two methodologies: -

1. The Walkthrough; and
2. The Deep Cleanse

The Deletion Walkthrough

To do this you will utilise an entire day so that you carry out your day as normal and when you see any reminder of us during this typical day, you delete without hesitation of prevarication (hence why it is very helpful to have a good friend accompany you with this task). Remember that we are structured and methodical in the manner by which we imbue Ever Presence and lay down the various triggers. You need to respond in a similar fashion.

If any of the items which need to be deleted belong to us, you should place them in a particular box or boxes and organise for a third party to return them to us. Do not damage or destroy those items no matter how tempting. If we learn that you have done this, we will use this as a basis of police complaint against you for criminal damage and use this as part of a smear campaign against you and/or a hoover. Do not return the items in person or ask us to pick them up. Arrange for someone else to attend to it. If need be leave them outside our front door if we will not take them back.

If the alarm that sounds to wake you is the same song or tone that would wake you when we were together, immediately change it.

When you wake up if your eyes alight on a picture of the two of us together on the nightstand, then remove that photograph. Tear it in two and as you do so say,

"(Name of narcissist) I delete you." Then place it in your refuse sack. Do this with every step of this deletion process.

Alternatively, place it in the Burn Box (see later)

If you see another picture on the wall of us, delete it. Do not walk past and think I will do it after I have used the bathroom. It must be done straight away.

In the bathroom if there are any toiletries, equipment and the like that we used (or used with you) remove them. You may even consider changing the toiletries that you use, especially if we used to comment about them – "I really like that Dolce e Gabanna perfume that you wear" or "I love the smell of that shampoo that you use."

Did we read a particular book when we used the bathroom, a magazine perhaps? Is it still there? Remove it. Did we use a specific towel that is readily identifiable? Remove it.

When you get dressed are there any of our clothes still in the wardrobe hung up, lying on the floor, on top of the wardrobe etc.? If so remove them. Are there any clothes or shoes that we purchased as gifts for you? Remove them.

With all of the items that you accumulate during this Deletion Walkthrough you have a choice: -

A Tear them up, cut them up, squash them, break them, shatter them and dispose of them;

b. Put them in the Burn Box in readiness for a symbolic and purifying bonfire; and/or

c. Sell them, donate them to charity or give them away.

Once you have attended to your ablutions in the bathroom and got dressed, consider if anything from your make-up should be removed. Perhaps it is time for you to treat yourself to some new make-up. The same goes for toiletries and clothing.

Look at the bed. Does the duvet cover signify anything of us? If so, remove it. Clear out our nightstand.

Head downstairs for breakfast. If there is anything that you see as you walk along the landing and down the stairs which is related to us, remove it.

In the kitchen, make your usual breakfast and as you do so consider if there is anything which is a reminder of us. Perhaps it is a particular breakfast cereal that we ate, if so, get rid of it. Was there a certain brand of juice we liked to drink? If so, remove it and change brands if you liked it as well.

I think you are getting the picture. At this point have your friend join you and together go through your normal routine in and around the house for a typical day. Include going to the shops, the gym, other interests and also if going to work if applicable. You need to adopt the mind set through this day of,

"What reminds me of the narcissist?"

It will be difficult for you because it will be highly emotional. It will be difficult because you will need to delete items which you have an emotional attachment to, items which may be financially valuable and you actually like but in order to effect the exorcism effectively you must be vigorous and ruthless in your approach. You need to reduce to the lowest level you can, the existence of the Causal Actions which result in the Aftermath Effects. Part of achieving this is to undertake a thorough Walkthrough Deletion whereby you follow your usual day and at each step you consider what is (or might) trigger a thought or memory about us and then you remove that item. Take the entire day to do it as different memories will be associated with different times of the day and different activities which occur at those different times. Ensure that your friend knows to be firm with you so that there is no deviation. There can be no excuse for keeping anything, not if you want execute a successful exorcism. Everything must go. Do not allow any excuses such as: -

"It is expensive."

"It is one of a kind."

"It was from when we were happy together."

"It seems a shame to waste it."

"I will miss it."

"How about I keep one and get rid of the rest?"

"But it such a lovely photograph."

No excuses. No hesitation. No ifs and no buts. Delete anything and everything which has any kind of link to us.

You may need to adopt this walkthrough approach two or three times. Perhaps once for a weekday and another for the weekend so that each action you would normally take (and which you will be repeating as your life moves forward) is divested of any infection from us.

The Deep Cleanse

Once the Walkthrough Deletion has taken place a few days later you need to set time aside for the Deep Cleanse. Again utilise the assistance of a friend (or even friends) for the purposes of considering as many scenarios as possible which may trigger a recollection.

For instance, if we always sat in a certain place in the sitting room, move the furniture around to disrupt the image that is automatically conjured up. You cannot delete your sitting room (unless of course you move properties and that is often just not feasible) but you can delete the image associated with it. Consider re-decorating where appropriate and work through the house once again, standing in different places in rooms to see if any images of us persist. If they do, consider how you can then remove that image by making appropriate changes.

Ensure that all gifts and tokens provided by us are removed.

Any handwritten items created by us or you should be considered and deleted.

Work through electronic storage. Purge any evidence of us from online sources. As part of no contact you are best placed by shutting down your online presence even if only for a few months, but you need to ensure that laptops, PCs, 'phones, tablets etc. have no pictorial or written evidence. Again you cannot allow anything to remain.

Ask your friend or friends what they consider might provide a link to us. It is always helpful to obtain additional perspectives as part of this process. The Deep Cleanse is a through sweeping through all elements of your life to ensure that no corner or crevice is untouched. If there are items at your family's houses they need to be removed as well. If friends have trigger items ask them to delete them in the same way, take down pictures on social media, remove comments referring to us and so forth.

You also need to work with your supporters to consider the places that are associated with us and thus might prove to be a trigger of the Aftermath Effects. Draw up a list of all the places that have an association to us – where we live, where we work, the bars, the restaurants, the church, the cinema, the shops, the gym, the stadium, the friends' houses and so on. Create a blacklist so that you know to avoid all of these places. The approach to this black list will form part of your Preventative Maintenance (see below).

Once the Walkthrough Deletion and the Deep Cleanse have been undertaken you will find yourself with: -

a. Several refuse sacks of material to take to the tip;

b. Items to be returned to us;

c. Items to sell if you so choose (have a friend deal with this on your behalf for a cut of the proceeds so you are not hanging on to items until they are sold)

d. A Burn Box with material if you chose this option as well.

You will also have a much tidier house!

If you have a Burn Box then organise a bonfire, invite trusted friends and enjoy a drink and something to eat as you allow a cleansing and purifying fire to consume those items which you placed in the Burn Box. You will find the process of seeing those reminders being consumed by flames, blacken and turn to dust extremely cathartic.

The removal of the items and/or the bonfire will be the final act of the process of deletion. It will have been emotional in dealing with all of these memories in such a short space of time but you have purged them, you have deleted them. Not only have you massively reduced the incidences of potential Ever Presence et al, you will have adjusted your thinking and engaged in a cathartic act which will acts as firebreak between what you have endured and going forward.

Preventative Maintenance

This is an ongoing part of the process going forward as the conduct of your exorcism is not a one-off event but an ongoing process. Whilst you have deleted much that could act as triggers, you will not be able to eradicate everything and also certain instances cannot be eradicated, instead, they must be dealt with by way of reduction and evasion.

By altering your thinking and undergoing the deletion you will have begun to train your mind to respond in a certain way to potential triggers. Rather than being consumed by emotion initially, you will respond in a defensive manner first. The emotion will follow but if you can activate a successful defence first then you will head the emotion off before it has a chance to envelope you.

For example, there will be certain songs which are strongly associated with us. You will have deleted those songs from your iTunes catalogue and removed them from your iPod and iPhone etc. However there remains a risk that you might hear the song on your radio or whilst in a bar. In those instances, you will react by not allowing yourself to wallow and listen to the song, but instead you will switch off the radio or leave the bar, or talk to someone so you are not listening to it. Eventually, you will do this as an instinctive reaction with the result that one day that particular song will play and you will not react to it in an emotional manner because you have conditioned yourself not to respond. You may not even realise that it has been played or if you do, you will realise that you felt nothing and that is a huge recognition of the progress you have made and that your exorcism of us is proving effective.

Preventative maintenance is a mind-set which you need to adopt as you move forward. You need to think that if a reminder, a trigger, or a memory appears how can you address it straight away. It might be to engage in a distraction (as mentioned above), it might be to remove yourself from a place, it may be to change channels or switch a device off.

During the Deep Cleanse you will have compiled a location blacklist. With this blacklist you need to apply this in terms of: -

A. Avoiding those places altogether;

B. Identifying alternatives which you can go to;

C. Avoiding those places initially until you feel strong enough to go to them for the purpose of creating New Associations (see below)

Knowing in advance the places where me might be or which are associated with us enables you to avoid triggers and also has the residual benefit of enabling you to reduce the risk of being hoovered.

The application of Preventative Maintenance is an ongoing process which you will need to train your mind to adopt but after a while it will become second nature to you. The mantra to adopt during this is

Avoid

Reduce

Minimise

Evade

Diminish

This is A.R.M.E.D.

By applying A.R.M.E.D. to each and every day you will ensure that those triggers which you might have forgotten about or more likely those which you cannot stop, can be nullified in terms of their effect on you.

Distraction

I have mentioned above about how you must discipline your mind so that if you begin to think about us you will cast out that thought as quickly as possible before the emotion takes hold.

You also need to apply a different form of distraction.

In the aftermath of an entanglement with our kind you will have the following problems: -

- A lack of desire to do anything so that you in effect mope and wallow, so this allows you to have more time to be at risk of thinking about us;
- We will have isolated you so that you will have lost certain networks and connections which would otherwise support you and distract you, thus you have more time alone and accordingly you are at a greater risk of thinking about us;
- We engineered a situation where most of your time was spent with us and now we have gone. Not only does this hole mean you are susceptible to thinking about us, you also have the double difficulty because you will be prone to thinking,

"It is Sunday evening; we always went for a walk down by the river at this time."

"It's Thursday. This was when we went to the Italian for dinner every week."

These are the Vulnerable Moments.

- We will have caused you to give up interests and hobbies external to our relationship as part of our control of you.

You need to fill this time. This will reduce the risk of thinking about us and in turn by doing something you enjoy, something that is about you, you will be able to rebuild your self-wroth and self-esteem by looking out for yourself. The more time you do something other than think about us, the less you will think about us, until over time the cumulative effect of this will cause you to say,

"I cannot remember before now when it was the last time I thought about him or her."

That will be a watershed moment for you.

Accordingly, you need distractions: -

- Rekindle friendships
- See your family more
- Take up those hobbies again
- Start a new hobby
- Opt to lose weight or get fitter;
- Learn a new language
- Go to places you have not been before;
- Start a home improvement project;
- Decide to tackle the works of a new author or director

Whatever it is look to fill your time and specially to fill those Vulnerable Moments so you stop thinking, "This time was when we would always do the shopping together" and instead it will be "It's time for my fine art class."

You allowed us to occupy your time and your mind. You are seizing control back and through this exorcism you are occupying your mind and your time with you, not us.

Overthrow the Totalitarian Regime

As I have just mentioned, you were occupied by an invading force. You have been infected and in order to carry out this exorcism you need to overthrow this totalitarian regime, this regime being a particular mind-set. As part of this overthrow, which forms part of the overall exorcism, you need to: -

- Engage in thought substitution in your favour. We did this. We through the Causal Actions and Aftermath Effects have made you always think of us. You now need to forget about what was apparently wonderful about us (because it was not real and it was all based on lies) and instead focus on your accomplishments and achievements. Those are not just those in your day to day life but the accomplishments you secure as part of this ongoing exorcism;

- Understand that much of why you were manipulated was to either exploit vulnerabilities which arose in your childhood (which causes you to be drawn to our kind) or it is designed to treat you as a child. You are made to think and feel like you are child by our treatment of you. You are not a child but an adult who is able to take action and makes choices.

- Remove Eternity Thinking. This is a situation where you think that nothing will change and you will always feel like this, always be treated like this and that you cannot move forward. Naturally our treatment of you is to make you think like this and keep you thinking like this. By engaging in Eternity Thinking all you are doing is perpetuating the current state of affairs. This is not productive for you. Remind yourself that this will not last forever, that you are making progress and indeed you have taken a huge step forward as a consequence of reading and following the principles in this book. You have increased your understanding and improved you prospects of driving us from you.

- Remember you have your own boundaries which you are asserting through this exorcism and the implementation of no contact. Reinforcing these boundaries will give you a sense of grounding and lessen that sensation of being out of control which only serves to increase your sense of anxiety and paralysis.

New Associations

The creation of New Associations is an integral and important part of you being able to not only do those things you once enjoyed again without the pain and misery of our toxic influence, but it is also a statement of intent. It is telling out kind that we did not win. That you have not lost your way, that you have not been prevented from doing the things you like and are important to you. As I explained, as part of Preventative Maintenance you will avoid certain places and doing certain things because of the trigger effect. As you feel yourself becoming stronger (and you will) you can then address these places and situations in order to overlay new memories so that when you think of that Thai restaurant you remember the raucous night you had with friends there rather than us.

In creating these New Associations be selective. You cannot hope to over write every single thing that you and I once did together. There are two reasons why that is not sustainable: -

1. Our laying down of triggers and Ever Presence was so extensive there is a lot for you to address which will distract you from performing the exorcism effectively. You only have so much time and energy; and

2. You will spread the over-writing too thinly and not obliterate the memories associated with us.

Accordingly, identify those places and events which are the most special to you and which you would not rather lose to deletion and the location blacklist. I would suggest no more than ten. Once identified you can then make arrangements with supporters, family and even new people that you have met to go to these places and to do so regularly so that they become associated with different people and different experiences and not with us. Again it will take time to achieve this and if you do not believe you are able to do it, do not do it, you are not ready. You will know when you feel able (as your exorcism continues and becomes more and more effective) so that you will then decide that you will visit your favourite castle with your best friend or you will attend the race meeting with a group of friends. By doing his and creating these new experiences you will cause your thinking to alter so that you will eventually link these new places with the new experiences and now with us. Our ghost is steadily being eradicated and exorcised.

Adopt Realism

This will not happen overnight. The exorcism is an ongoing process. The laying down of triggers, the creation of Ever Presence, the formation of the After Effect Questions all happened over time when you were not aware of what was going on. We did not cause them straight away but instead did so through the steady application of repetitive conduct which reinforced these action and their effects. In the same way as we layered them on to you, you must take time to strip back layer after layer as you move forward. You will make progress and then you may plateau for a period of time, you may even slide back a little, but by repeating your understanding of the principles as to how it has happened to you and adopting the application of the constructive steps you can take to achieve your exorcism then you will make progress. It will take weeks and months but you will notice the improvements and it is akin to pushing a boulder. At first it is very difficult as you attempt to overcome inertia, but once it starts going it becomes easier as the cumulative effect of your understanding and the constructive steps mesh together so that your exorcism comes to fruition. Be patient, understand it will take time because you are fighting the battle against emotion and then engaging in the battle of head against heart, but by following what I have written you will succeed. I know.

Avoid Seeking Answers from Unproductive Sources

Part of the reason why you are unable to move forward is your desire to obtain answers. That is understandable and part of what we engineer. You want answers and therefore you will seek them from: -

- Us
- Family
- Friends
- Supposed experts
- Anybody who will listen

All of those categories are potentially unproductive sources.

We will not help you (apart from what I write here and in my other books – there is where the answers lie_) because we will want to hoover you and to keep you dangling, guessing and wondering. You may think that we will give you answers; we will probably promise to do so but you will not get them from us. It will not serve our purposes.

- Family are well meaning but they are most unlikely to understand what you are dealing with. They can provide support in many ways but they will not have the answers.
- Friends. The same as with families
- There are experts who have answers for you but finding those who actually understand what you have experienced is often harder than you think. Be wary of certain forums which may appear to provide answers but are really places where the same behaviours are described, railed against and lambasted but there is no constructive provision of answers. These are just wallowing holes. Like a waterhole attracts animals, the wallowing hole attracts lots of victims buts rarely anybody with the answers that you need;

- Your desperation will have you talking about your experience with anybody who will listen. They will not have the answers.

By going to the wrong place all you will do is become frustrated and end up replaying what has happened to you over and over again. This will not allow you to exorcise us from your heart and soul. Instead all you are doing is allowing us to remain there and indeed embed ourselves deeper.

Maintain No Contact

No Contact provides you with a raft of benefits. You should have it in place (or as near as you can achieve subject to circumstances) prior to commencing your exorcism. Do not let No Contact fail (or if it does start it again) as it provides the bedrock and many residual benefits for making your exorcism effective. You can read my insights about this in **No Contact: How to Beat the Narcissist.**

I always remind people that the key to achieving freedom is to understand. You now understand how you become infected, how we achieve this, why it is so effective and the effects it has on you. By gaining this understanding you straight away remove a considerable disadvantage and advance your prospects of success. Not knowing (especially to an empathic individual who needs to know) creates distress, fear, anxiety and a feeling of helplessness. One of the biggest weapons our kind has against you is that you rarely understand why we do what we do. My writing is giving you that understanding and therefore this in itself provides you with a massive advantage in purging us.

You also now know how the very things which hold you back and pain you, the Aftermath Effects can be tackled because I have detailed various constructive methodologies above which are specific to diminishing and then extinguishing the Aftermath Effects and who can know better than the very person who put them there in the first place?

You now have what you need to purge the narcissist who has infected you, from your heart and soul, as part of your ongoing recovery from your entanglement with our kind.

Further required reading from H G Tudor

Evil

Narcissist: Seduction

Narcissist: Ensnared

Manipulated

Confessions of a Narcissist

More Confessions of a Narcissist

Further Confessions of a Narcissist

From the Mouth of a Narcissist

Escape: How to Beat the Narcissist

Danger: 50 Things You Should Not Do with a Narcissist

Departure Imminent: Preparing for No Contact to beat the Narcissist

Fuel

Chained: The Narcissist's Co-Dependent

A Delinquent Mind

Fury

Beautiful and Barbaric

The Devil's Toolkit

Sex and the Narcissist

Treasured and Tormented

No Contact: How to Beat the Narcissist

Revenge: How to Beat the Narcissist

Adored and Abhorred

Sitting Target: How and Why the Narcissist Chooses You

Black Hole: The Narcissistic Hoover

A Grimoire of Narcissism

Cherished and Chastised

Red Flag: 50 Warning Signs of Narcissistic Seduction

Ask the Narcissist: The Answers to Your Questions

Darlings and Demons

Black Flag: 50 Warning Signs of Abuse

Your Fault: Blame and the Narcissist

Elated and Eroded

Outnumber Not Outgunned

Deciphered: What the Narcissist Really Means

Feted and Feared

Smeared: Knowing and Beating the Narcissist's Campaign

Ghosted and Gilded

Why? Understanding the Narcissist's Behaviour

All available on Amazon

Further interaction with H G Tudor

Knowing the Narcissist

@narcissist_me

Facebook

Narcsite.wordpress.com

Made in the USA
San Bernardino, CA
29 November 2017